Architectural Association London
AA Agendas No. 11

Mediating
Architecture

*Edited by Theo Lorenz
& Peter Staub*

AA Agendas No. 11

Mediating Architecture

Edited by Theo Lorenz & Peter Staub
AA Agendas Series Editor: Brett Steele
AA Art Director: Zak Kyes
Design: Claire McManus
Photography: Sue Barr, Valerie Bennett and Diploma Unit 14

AA Publications are produced
through the AA Print Studio
aaprintstudio.net

Printed in Belgium by Cassochrome

ISBN 978-1-902902-71-5

To order a catalogue of AA Publications
or specific titles visit aaschool.ac.uk/publications
or email publications@aaschool.ac.uk

AA Publications
36 Bedford Square
London WC1B 3ES
T + 44 (0)20 7887 4021
F + 44 (0)20 7414 0783

Cover: Thames Gateway Assembly exhibition, AA Gallery 2006.
Photo Valerie Bennett

Contents

Space vs Interface: From Architectural Media to (its) Matter

Brett Steele

Most bad habits are tools to help us through life.
– Friedrich Nietzsche

Modern architectural histories that privilege the role of architectural media in the forming of architectural imagination largely await contemporary revision – at least, so as to make them able to more fully comprehend, and then convincingly situate, the arrival and rapid assimilation of late modern 'new' media in the architect's studio and, more importantly, in the larger, historical context of architectural knowledge.

What has the still relatively recent electronic dispersal of hard and soft design systems and platforms within, across and very much beyond the architect's studio really coincided with? Surely something more than the arrival of the car-wreck curvilinear formalism of so many a youthful enthusiast of digital design platforms? Most likely, given the inevitable effects of new tools on the human mind, we can expect the consequence to be something greater than the shape of buildings.

A profound revolution amongst a younger generation of architects is unfolding today within minds that increasingly conceive of architecture and its core disciplinary problems not in terms of space, but rather (and here's the twist) as interface. In these early years of a new century space vs interface is already proving itself as an architectural battle for the ages. These two increasingly competitive (if not outright antagonistic) terms situate themselves in architectural minds being formed, above all, through a relentless daily experience of both: space and interface. In profound ways, the idea of an interface is presenting itself with a force able to rewrite the history, and not only presence, of a discipline still all-too-expectant of (if not outright comfortable with) a modern idea of space. Over recent decades the story has held, but mostly and only if we look to what architects produce or say, rather than how they have long worked (work that has been carried out via perspectival machines, rendering conventions, geometries and other artifices whose most shared characteristic is the manipulation of symbolic information as an interface – whether it be a blank sheet of paper or a coded diagram).

For centuries the organisation of form in matter, the structuring of built space, has been central to the architect's very conception of architectural knowledge. The making of architectural space has been literally (and not only literarily, since the invention of architectural books) the definition of architecture and the purpose of architectural mental and manual labour. In earlier eras, classical space was a matter of orderly composition, whose principles were the stuff of books, encyclopaedia and trained method. A century ago a revolution of a distinctly modern and experimental kind shifted the terms and appearances of architectural space and form, but not its larger disciplinary emphasis on space and form (a fact startlingly revealed for many architects in the mid-twentieth-century forensics of Rowe and others, with a demonstration of the hidden conspiracies connecting villas by Le Corbusier with those by Palladio four centuries before).

This, of course, is where things are getting interesting today, when we come to speculate on the consequences of (once new, increasingly ordinary) architectural media. For the first time in many decades today's changes have extended themselves knowingly to include a profound rearrangement of that one architectural space central to the invention of ideas about architectural space: the architect's own design studio. Which, if you haven't looked around lately, is starting to look and not only be treated much less like a space than an interface.

And this is the space/interface through which AA Diploma 14 has knowingly projected itself, initially in their speculation on what they call 'the design of design processes' within the studio and then, even more interestingly, in exploring the ways in which models of that space/interface become the very same models by which to approach complex, large-scale urban problems in contemporary London. These include projects like the Thames Gateway, the focus for many of the projects included here, whose greatest level of complexity is in the modelling of the very design processes already underway and nearly invisible, owing to the interaction of local, governmental, planning and regulatory participants.

In the work of AA Diploma 14 architecture's core problem involves the making of space (and/or interface) in terms of contemporary network theories, many of which are cited extensively in the essays accompanying these projects. It is the peculiar features of space within networks that give added urgency to the question of how we might understand the role of new, network-based media in relation to a contemporary architectural imagination. Because network space, whatever else it is, is surely different from the kind of space architects have long been expertly producing.

Yes, networks can be seen to have space (contemporary network sciences seek to explore, model and understand these precisely), but the kind of space they have, we would all agree, is most certainly different than the kind found in a Borromini church or a villa by Le Corbusier. Likewise, architectural or urban space can be modelled or conceived as if within or part of a network (of other spaces). This proto-approach features prominently in the history of modern architecture and urban planning (we see the sensibility articulated clearly in the early infrastructural modern town-planning efforts of Le Corbusier, in the work of Team Ten and their circulatory networks and mat buildings, as well as any number of other examples).

The difference today is a younger generation's growing awareness that networks and their spaces really aren't anything like those spaces architects or others understand when thinking of built form, and to treat the one as if the other is nonsense. The task is greater: to develop expertise in both. Indeed, in a world when an increasing portion of an architect's waking life is spent literally staring into an artificial interface of a new and unexpected kind (a display screen, a window within a program or other surfaces decidedly different from those drawn or perspectival interfaces of yesteryear), the question of space versus interface is becoming less abstract and more lived with each passing hour (or release of a new scripting language or protocol). More than a century ago the philosopher Friedrich Nietzsche, with failing eyesight and an unsteady, ageing hand, switched to the typewriter as a writing tool of choice (in current parlance, we would call him an 'early adopter'). His subsequent commentary and philosophical reflection on the effects this device had on his thought – much more important, he observed, than the mere effect it had on his writing – offers us early evidence of a most contemporary feeling: that our minds, architectural or otherwise, are being changed in ways we can hardly yet describe. To embrace the unexpected, and to seek to give appearance to the architecturally unseen – space, interface or otherwise – is what really drives the work included in *Mediating Architecture*. On behalf of the entire school, my thanks to everyone involved.

AADip14

Theo Lorenz

What's next? Architects are always searching for the next big solutions, but today these seem harder than ever to find or define. Perhaps we simply need to change our focus and concentrate on new forms of design rather than on hypothetical aims or ideals.

The role of architects has expanded in response to the incredible range of demands that must be met in today's built environment and the broad spread of specialisations inherent in contemporary professional practices. From being merely the designer of built artefacts, architects are becoming mediators within a network of complex concerns. This is a form of continuous mediation that takes place on multiple levels throughout the process of construction. It takes place between parties in the building industry, embedding logistical and material concerns within the negotiation of design; between the public, the clients and the designers, ensuring that any strategy or plan has both a public and private mandate; and finally between the actual design and its environment, displaying an awareness and management of both the silent ecological parties involved in any site and the 'afterlife' of a design. The work described in this publication explores this extended definition of an architect.

The topic of mediation and networking of the architectural process beyond the traditional confines of the discipline was central to the unit from the outset. A continuation of the work of Intermediate Unit 6 and Diploma Unit 9, which I had been teaching for five years together with John Bell, AADip14 was formed with Peter Staub and Neil Davidson in collaboration with Nina Power and Tanja Siems as an extended interdisciplinary team of architects, designers, landscape architects and urban planners bridging academia and practice, theoretical and applied concerns.

In this book we often refer to Bruno Latour and his theories. When we first invited Latour to the AA in 1998, he began his lecture by declaring that he did not know why an architectural school would be interested in him and that he initially did not know what to talk about, but that he might as well give it a try! He then proceeded to deliver an inspiring lecture on Paris through the notion of the polyopticon. Today he could no longer be so self-deprecating, as he publishes widely on architecture and urban design, often in collaboration with Peter Sloterdijk, and the extent of his influence is undeniable.

Given the multitude of influences and tasks involved in architecture and urban design, it becomes essential for architects to relate the various stakeholders and to restore a political dimension to the project as well as to anticipate the inevitable differences between the original concept and the actual realisation. All of these issues are discussed by Latour.

As architects we are concerned with objects, the architectural objects we design. According to the Actor Network Theory, we see that these objects do not exist in isolation but are part of assemblies consisting of both human and non-human agents or actants, with parameters that are constantly shifting and transforming. This can be best explained with one of Latour's most important ideas, the concept of the 'matter of concern' versus a 'matter of fact'. Latour claims that nothing can be seen as an indisputable matter of fact, as everything stands in relation to other things. When this relation changes, the 'facts' also shift. Latour therefore describes 'facts' as 'matters of concern' in which definitions depend on relations and links. In contrast to scientists, who try to discover matters of fact, architects seem to decide matters of fact a priori, even though their conjectures rarely turn out to be well-founded! However, according to Latour, designers should start to understand the design task as an overall process, constantly making connections in order to substantiate the overall design idea and create interventions that work as actants and mediators within the relevant networks.

In these systems of thought we cannot hide behind abstraction. We need to be able to clearly communicate the processes that make things happen. Through his own clear, precise style of writing, Latour teaches us that it is possible to demonstrate complicated matters intelligibly – even to 'visual' people like architects!

Based on an awareness that sooner or later architectural design will have to become mediated, the teaching of the unit was concerned to incorporate a process of negotiation from the very outset. It was our aim to educate the students to realise a series of engaged, networked projects. Rather than being pushed to follow any formal trend that happened to be in vogue, students were encouraged to be flexible enough to allow for the necessary transformations within the architectural design. This way of working, with its constant oscillations between academia and applied practice, is quite demanding, since students have to be able to coordinate and manage their designs while also continually elaborating, communicating and mediating feedback into the wider strategy of the applied project. Nevertheless, reality asks even more of architects and those involved in creative industries. Therefore, it was a constant aim of the unit to teach the students to be able to react to and find richness in situations whose normal state is that of flux, instead of being specially trained in the programmes of the day to reproduce the latest de rigueur shape.

This could be seen as a 'post-digital' approach, an approach that does not describe a time without digital technology but rather claims that the digital is no longer accepted as an end in itself. The excitement once generated by digital processing is long gone. We have instead started to ask: 'digital, and...? What do we do with it, how does it change, how can it have an after-effect and how is it manifested?' Merely processing parameters is not enough. However it is obvious that we cannot (nor would we want to) revert to the analogue alone, as any analogue action will always acknowledge the presence of the digital, merge with it and become something new! The new generation of designers should aspire to a virtuoso use of both procedures, in constant exchange.

In this way the unit work never concentrates on one specific mode of representation or selection of softwares, tools or even a single style; rather it is about a mode of working and the ability to learn and combine the appropriate method at any given moment. At the outset of their careers, the students were thus enabled to work within this extended definition of the discipline, equipped with the knowledge of how to initiate and realise their own projects and networks – skills that allowed them to see alternatives to working within the established institutions of the profession.

Diploma Unit 9 (John Bell and Theo Lorenz), Duplicity 1 at Battersea Power Station, 2004

Diploma Unit 9 (John Bell and Theo Lorenz), Duplicity 2 at the AA, 2005

Design of the Design Process

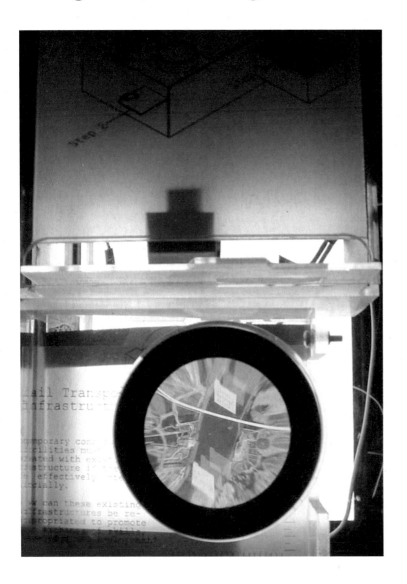

Design of the Design Process

Theo Lorenz

This division between objectivity and subjectivity ensures that one cannot
simultaneously concentrate on both, the big and the small, the real and the
symbolic, the human and nonhuman, the scientific and the 'vécu'. Thus, the
traditional optics of our mental camera force us to choose between foreground
and background, without ever being able to have the two sharply in focus at
the same time.[1]

The popular image of the architect is still tinged by memories of Howard Roark in
the book of Ayn Rand's *The Fountainhead* (1949). A young man has to struggle to realise
'his' ideal building – defying conservative clients and outdated traditions, he remains
faithful to his values and prevails at last. In this view an architect can only create if he
makes no compromises. Any changes to his ideals would ultimately lead to their
destruction, any alteration is seen as a loss. The resulting structure should be faithful to
the original concept, even if the world may have changed significantly during the long
development of a building that was, naturally, far ahead of its time! The decisions of the
architect are regarded as justified 'a priori', and so are seen as indisputable.

Today, this image is obviously outdated. We all know that architecture has to
undergo a process of development and that we have to make some compromises along
the way. Nevertheless, if we are honest, most young architects still dream of the big
competition win and the ideal client who will let them do just what they want, without
compromises. Most architecture students look up to the handful of 'star architects' who
build all over the world in their own 'signature' style.

Today it is of course not enough to argue for a design on the bases of 'taste' or
purity of form and function, as the fictional 'modernist' architect Howard Roark might
have done. Today the facts are created through a multitude of parameters. The design and
forms of buildings are created by parametric tools integrating important environmental,
social and geometric considerations. These tools allow designers to choose from a huge
palette of possibilities, achieving designs that are more complex and carefully rehearsed
than would be possible when following a single person's 'ideal'. Nevertheless this design
methodology is still aiming at a definitive outcome justified by a collection of 'facts'. The
fabrication of facts, often disguised as research, can take up the longest time within the
process, simply to ensure that the resulting design is beyond any doubt. The architecture
is based on scientific claims and indubitable facts, and thus the design itself has to be the
product of a logical development.

However, if we look at the presentation of architectural designs in pristine white
models and images of shiny cities with green trees and happy people, we see hardly any
resemblance with built structures. Even if designers and architects are better equipped
today than ever before, at the same time they are faced with growing numbers of
restrictions, liabilities and limitations which seem to disarm their aspirations from the
outset. In this situation the architect must have knowledge that extends far beyond the
'building' process, gained either through individual effort or by intense networking beyond
the profession. Architecture without compromise seems impossible. Even in the 'best-case'
scenario, with a satisfied client and planning authority, the building process itself is so s
low that by the time the project is finished it is already outdated, resulting in a very short
lifespan for contemporary architecture.

1. Bruno Latour, '"Air-condition": Our New
    Political Fate', *Domus*, March 2004.

The problems in this scenario arise less from the design itself, or from anyone's ambitions, and more from the overall attitude towards change and transformation. As long as the basic parameter of design is to 'allow as little negotiation as possible', and any change is seen as a 'compromise' diminishing the original idea, architects can only be disappointed with the outcome.

It seems that we are confronted with a difficult dilemma, but once we recognise that an 'a priori' design is an illusion we can redirect our creative energy towards a design that invites negotiation and transformation throughout its entire process. This reversal of the relationship between the design and the 'final' outcome is not a radical departure from architects' methods or objectives but simply a change of perspective. If the eventual building is not seen as the sole aim of the spatial design, the architectural design itself can become the motor and inspiration for its own development.

However, this change of approach opens up a series of new questions and possibilities for the profession. A whole area of design is there to be claimed by the architect: the design of the design process. This is, of course, quite distinct from simply establishing a time frame for the construction process that makes provision for the unexpected. It involves the mediation of the design and all aspects of its communication and representation, a procedure that becomes a core part of the architectural work itself. Anticipating that there will be departures from the initial design, we can see that the basis of negotiation has changed from the notion that the object of architecture is a matter of fact towards Bruno Latour's notion of the 'matter of concern'.[2]

Latour believes nothing can be described as an 'undisputed fact';[3] rather, everything should be seen as part of an assembly within which it has value. It is important to determine how one can continually describe these shifting values within the overall assembly. In terms of architecture this means that the whole assembly, together with its transformative qualities, becomes the architectural project, and not just the built structure. In other words each step of the design is always a project in itself, judged not by its eventual product but by its ability to initiate its own next transformation.

This puts into question the definition of what an architectural realisation might be. If the 'final design' can no longer be seen as a matter of fact, any form of the project can be regarded as a realisation, as long as it is consistent with Latour's notion of a 'matter of concern'. Within this definition of architecture the designed artefact is not the only possible outcome of the process. It is instead a tool of negotiation that results in a spatial transformation. By focusing on a project's actual effect within the spatial environment, rather than solely on its built form, each formation of the project, whether it is a drawing, a model, an exhibition or temporary constructions, becomes a design task involving a process of mediation.

Therefore it can be seen that each project has multiple parallel outcomes and aims which complement each other but are not necessarily interdependent, as they form overlapping networks of matters of concern. The importance and influence of each design phase thus expands immensely, opening up new fields of work for architects. If the realisation of a project is defined by its consequences, its lasting effects on relevant stakeholders and on the next phase of the overall project, each step of the design process stops being hypothetical. If a presentation of a design has an influence on the spatial environment, whether through activities, or by changing the cultural atmosphere or even specific policies, it becomes real and a project in its own right, triggering the emergence of further projects. Architecture here is no longer a single product but a series of interrelated products in the form of an assembly. Here the built form becomes by default one of many products, even though it might have been the driving factor that began the overall process.

2. Bruno Latour, 'Why Has Critique Run out of Steam? From Matters of Fact to Matters of Concern', *Critical Inquiry*, Winter 2004, 25–248.

3. The issue has been discussed by Latour in 'Making Things Public', in *From Realpolitik to Dingpolitik – or How to Make Things Public* (Cambridge, MA: MIT Press, 2005).

This is of course very demanding of the architect. Traditionally, architects produce two sets of reduced presentations of their projects: seemingly objective drawings in plan and section and subjective renderings, animations and physical models. All these media are inevitably partial and incomplete. To avoid such distinctions between the objective and subjective, the architect needs to develop mediating instruments – hybridised media tools that are capable of communicating design spatially across varying scales. This will allow stakeholders to participate and interact, enabling the gradual transformation of the original design into sustainable architecture on multiple levels. If we invite every stakeholder in a project to understand the important connections in the process, we enable them to take the project forward in a variety of directions, going beyond a conventional representation, which only allows an objective total view or a subjective partial impression.

This form of participation differs from conventional practice. In most cases participation means nothing but informing the various stakeholders to varying degrees about decisions already made. The stakeholders have to subscribe to the given standards of the practice and have to believe the visual impressions given to them. They must, therefore, be able to interpret these representations and have in most cases only the chance to agree or to disagree. However, if the participation allows stakeholders to be part of an actual, current realisation, their involvement and the consequences for subsequent phases of the project are exponentially more significant.

To apply this methodology of 'designing the design process', one does not need to reinvent practice, but rather appropriate and combine already existing and emerging techniques both from within the profession and from other creative fields. It is important not to adopt one method of working or a single approach through computing and parametric design. To create a negotiable process we need to use the whole range of possibilities of design and mediation. Computerised and digital work are neither privileged nor denied but instead are treated as a given set of opportunities, having been in existence for long enough to be both established media while not being the only possible mode of innovation. The designer should not be limited by his skill with computer technology, but rather should use those tools which are at hand, delegate an overall approach, and update his/her network of techniques constantly. With this post-digital approach we can use, misuse, combine and appropriate these techniques, and alternate between digital and analogue, virtual and real space.

From the very first presentation of the design, as early as the first sketch or a work model, to its built form, the key to the success of the project is its ability to mediate. This involves going beyond (but not necessarily excluding) traditional forms of representation in plans, sections and details, and 'visualisations' that focus on the structure in its assembled form, to demonstrations of the building's internal and external connections in both their physical and organisational aspects.

A widely known form of representation for assembly and assemblage is the exploded axonometric, which is commonly used within mechanics and product design but rarely employed by architects. Nevertheless, a single exploded axonometric can reveal connections between the different parts of a project, conveying aspects of time and sequence and configuration, and can be easily understood by laymen. One example of this would be the banal diagrams of IKEA furniture, which are designed to show consumers how to assemble the product. More sophisticated versions include representations of car engines or of Shimano bicycle gears. If we add human participants to the drawing, we begin to have a network representation of the building process, showing not merely the links between the different parts, but also the possibilities of transformation, reconnection and exclusion. The spectator can at all times zoom from the overall picture to specific parts, focus on specific types of actors, and visualise new possibilities and connections. Rather than a collection of loosely linked entities, networks here should be seen as 'worknets', as described by Bruno Latour in his Actor Network Theory.[4] Accordingly, what is important is not what is linked but what is actually 'at work' within an assembly.

The potential of these extended drawings can be applied even further if we start to use multidimensional techniques of representation, which take the form of hybrids between drawings and installations. These could be relief drawings, multi-layered showcases or installations that combine both digital and physical media. These representations have a spatial quality, inviting the spectator to change perspective and to move around the different configurations, as in Cornelia Parker's frozen installation of an exploding hut. In this way, the user becomes immersed within the assembly, understanding otherwise hidden relationships in hierarchy and time.

The components of these assemblies do not have to be limited to the physical content of a project but can extend to human stakeholders and policy. Information that usually has to be found in extensive documents and tedious files and folders, or which is just assumed to be known by the spectator, should be visible and accessible at a glance. Different stakeholders are all too frequently unaware of others within the network, and thus work in different directions or even against each other. Likewise, in most projects, the design is only checked against regulations and policies after it has been developed, even though these rules have a greater influence on a project's success than formal ideas and functionality. In most cases they are seen as an obstacle; they are hardly ever used – or misused – as a design tool. An immediate awareness of these issues is essential if the design process is to be based on negotiation rather than compromise. However, to be able either to misuse or to appropriate something more effectively, one must first be aware of it and learn to see it in its specific context. In most cases, if one is aware early enough of the specific relations and conditions, a design can offer a solution to the seemingly opposing elements of a project.

It is not enough merely to show the different stakeholders within the representation of the design, since these are continually changing throughout the entire process. Instead, presentations should be updated by means of logging and interaction, so that they start to become participatory design tools offering stakeholders a means of negotiation.

These methods of representation appear to be most successful when combined as interactive platforms for designs or built assemblies. The forms that these manifestations can take vary immensely, ranging from digital platforms to designed activities and playful collaborations, which can be as effective and even more direct than other media. A simple but powerful example of logging an opinion through a design is the installation by Lucy Kimbell and Andrew Barry at the 'Making Things Public' exhibition in Karlsruhe in 2005. In parallel perspex tubes, coloured buttons with varying statements were displayed. Visitors could take any of the buttons that they liked and agreed with. Obviously, the emptiest tube was the most popular, but at the same time each individual publicised the idea to which they subscribed by wearing the button. So one simple installation functioned both as an empirical record of public opinion and as a form of advertising.

Applied to spatial design, negotiation can itself leave traces within its applied environment. In both Celina Martinez-Cañavate's and Richa Mukhia's project within AADipl4, local participants and stakeholders were invited early in the design process to subscribe to a 'green' approach by distributing and cultivating plants, demonstrating a point of view whilst actually starting the greening of the city. In Richa's case, the initiatives became part of London's 'Green Grid' policy, leading to long-term design of public green space alongside local infrastructure.

4. Bruno Latour, 'On Recalling ANT', in John Law and John Hassard (eds), *Actor Network Theory and After* (Oxford, Blackwell, 1999).

The advantages of networking between places, stakeholders and information are obvious – perhaps so much so that there is a danger of the process being simplified and not used to its full potential. However, as John Law puts it,[5] every man, woman, child and dog seems to be talking of networks, and so their ability to aid mediation is of the utmost importance. The most significant aspect of digital design tools is that they can make specialised knowledge accessible, and hence usable and capable of being appropriated by non-experts. By using these tools, laymen can gain an insider's knowledge, as is particularly obvious in the case of advanced geometry software. While the underlying mathematics remain a mystery to most, knowledge about the context and content of the programmes is growing, allowing users to begin to script their own add-ons or applications.

If one extends this approach beyond the realm of a discipline to different stakeholders, a completely different set of knowledge has to be transferred, even more abstract to most people than mathematics is to architects and engineers. A good example of this is the work of Ekapob Suksudpaisarn. He developed a collaborative urban design tool which integrated structural and urban policies of a London site into an interactive platform that allowed even high school students to develop testable and discussable designs. The project's initial 'style' could be defined by a designer at the outset, but the resulting urban configuration was influenced by the stakeholders within the network. The project did not only work in relation to one specific project, but was further developed by Ekapob years after his diploma with various international players in architectural research, such as the urban research team of SOM and Google networks.

Mediating architecture unfolds its potential most prominently when both the virtual and the real start to merge, and the project can be developed in equilibrium between ephemerality and permanence, as is often the case in exhibitions and spatial installations. These spaces become assemblies, being able to capture technological and stylistic trends as well as current socio-political conditions. As they are not seen as final spaces, they can create a neutral ground of discussion between the different stakeholders, whilst being public at all times. In this environment various ideas can be tested and applied simultaneously. Unusual and unexpected combinations can happen, creating new alliances while generating new energy for ongoing processes. This became very apparent at the various shows made by AADip14, as well its predecessor Diploma Unit 9. In the 2005 'Duplicity' exhibition, curated by John Bell and myself, all the stakeholders of the Crystal Palace Park design team were assembled for the first time, challenged and inspired by the unconventional approaches of the students. At the unit's Thames Gateway assembly exhibition in May 2006, the display served as a strategies room for the otherwise diverse projects, as well as a place for discussion and assembly for many other groups inside and outside the AA. As such, both exhibitions became actual, realised spaces whilst triggering new discussions, possibilities and even decisions.

The possibility of a mediating architecture can be extended beyond the construction of exhibitions. Once it is accepted that architecture needs to be mediated, and that elements of design need to be introduced earlier in the process, it becomes clear that most projects should have built constituents of different temporal durations to help the development of the later stages. A well-known example of such a project, even though it might have been born from very different ambitions, is that of the 'info box' in Berlin by Schneider and Schumacher. The building was constructed as a showcase for the huge urban development of the Potsdamer Platz in Berlin. Acknowledging that the development would take a long time, and would arouse much controversy, the building was constructed long before the

5.   John Law, 'Networks, Relations, Cyborgs:
     On the Social Study of Technology',
     published by the Centre for Science Studies,
     Lancaster University and available at
     www.lancs.ac.uk/fass/sociology/papers/
     law-networks-relations-cyborgs.pdf

initiation of the development of the site overall, becoming the symbol of new architecture and urban development in Berlin. Whilst the site was changing around it from an urban void into a dense corporate environment, the 'info box' provided a destination for observing and speculating. Unfortunately here the opportunity was missed to have a real influence on the pre-existing masterplan.

Another example is that of a project within our own practice, as part of the Schweitzer Platz development by T2 in collaboration with B612 associates, currently under construction in Brussels. Here we were able to extend the contract to include a Media Pavilion. Instead of adding corporate pieces of public art at the end of the building process, we built a permanent media pavilion early on in the construction phase. Initially this is being used as a media centre for the participation process, introducing the project and its design, but later it will function as a local gathering point and framework for various media artists. These kinds of projects begin to combine permanent construction and mediation, creating overlaps and reversals of otherwise successive construction phases. Once these overlaps are created, the final project can no longer be seen as a final matter of fact, as it has itself already introduced and invited new transformations.

With the methodology of 'designing the design process', the mediation of architecture creates more design and more built architecture at an even earlier stage. It multiplies projects and allows architecture and design to have maximum impact. In ideal cases it creates not only more work for the architects but new paid commissions, which are viable for most clients as they minimise the risks of the overall project. Its products are multiple outcomes, leaving the client's options open rather than an 'all-or-nothing' approach that all too often leads to a complete re-start of the design process. Of course this methodology is not easily pinned down in terms of a style that can be repeated arbitrarily. Every process is different, and the designers involved can test their talent, taste and ability within the same methodology. This methodology offers every designer a mode of qualitative testing through a series of evolving realisations.

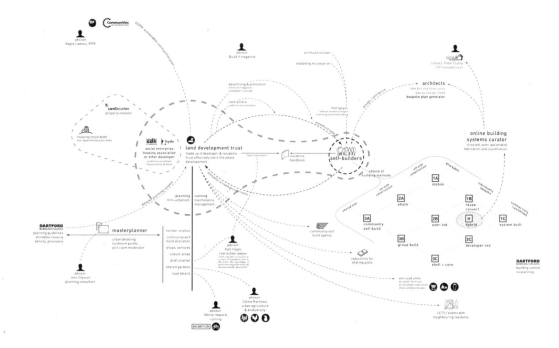

Levent Kerimol, social network diagram for self-build development project, 2007

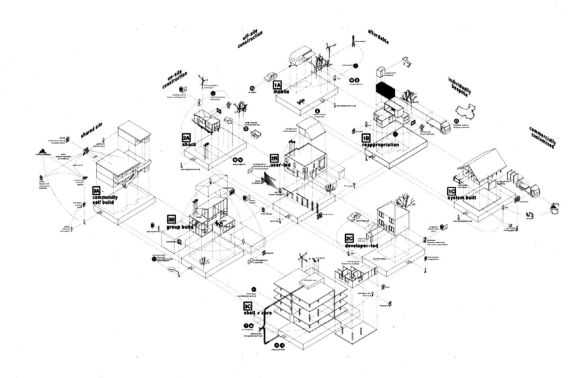

Levent Kerimol, network diagram for self-build development project combining social, economic and physical actants, 2007

the cycle line
housing+deck construction strategy

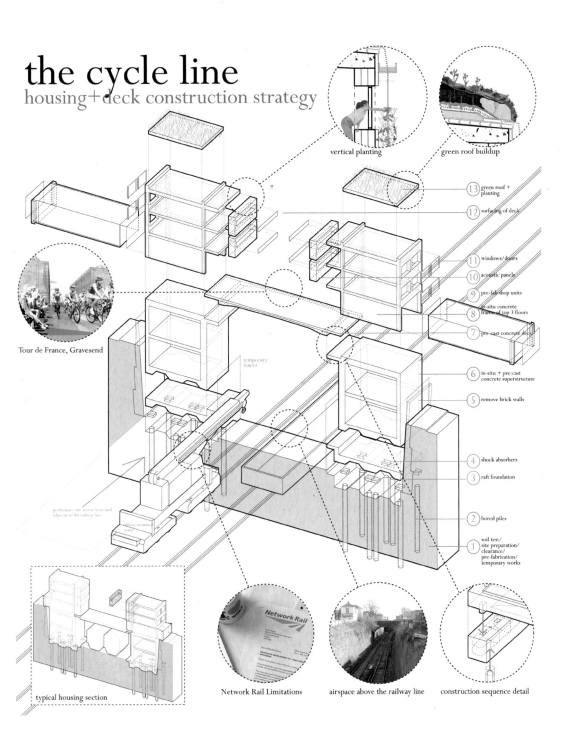

vertical planting

green roof buildup

Tour de France, Gravesend

13 green roof + planting

12 surfacing of deck

11 windows/doors

10 acoustic panels

9 pre-fab shop units

8 in-situ concrete frame of top 3 floors

7 pre-cast concrete deck

6 in-situ + pre-cast concrete superstructure

5 remove brick walls

4 shock absorbers

3 raft foundation

2 bored piles

1 soil test/ site preparation/ clearance/ pre-fabrication/ temporary works

typical housing section

Network Rail Limitations

airspace above the railway line

construction sequence detail

Mellis Haward, assembly drawing for the cycle line, 2008

19

Alex Thomas, design tools for Thames Gateway Bridge local education centre, 2006

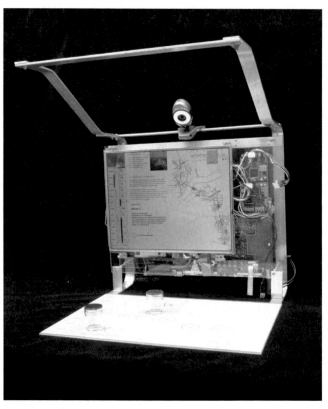

Max Babbe, design tool for slip road utilisation, 2006

Abi Tuttle, analogue design tool for contamination education, 2006

Esi Carboo, design tool for recycling station, 2006

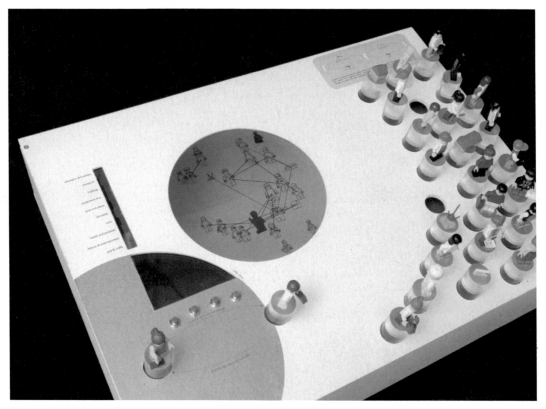

Levent Kerimol, design tool for local exchange trading scheme, 2006

Ben Burley, design tool for 'self-service [re]generation', displayed at the Brompton Design competition jury, 2007

Ekapob Suksudpaisarn, urban collaboration tool at the 'Guerilla Gateway' exhibition at the Kemistry Gallery, London, 2007

Strategy table, Thames Gateway Assembly exhibition at the AA Gallery, 2006

The strategy table allowed users to move planning elements within the study area

'Planning moves' on the strategy table triggered detailed information about the respective area or projects

Thames Gateway Assembly exhibition

Thames Gateway Assembly exhibition opening

Brompton Design competition jury, 2007

The Brompton Design competition jury assess the winning entry by Celina Martinez-Cañavate, 2007

Strategy table, Thames Gateway Assembly exhibition, 2006

Jury members Andrew Richie, John Worthington, Alex de Rijke, Tobias Goevert and Lisa Mackenzie with Alex Thomas's installation, 2007

The Brompton Design competition jury discuss the work of Nausica Gabrielides, 2007

Parliament of Architecture, X-D panels, 2008

Parliament of Architecture jury with Charles Tashima, Nina Power, Jonathan Laventhol, Tanja Siems and Christian Kuesters

Mediating Instruments:
Communicating Design

Mediating Instruments: Communicating Design

Peter Staub

What exactly is the role of the contemporary architect in a society preoccupied with the changing environment? Is he/she a designer, politician, communicator, eco-warrior or indeed all of the above? While some regard sustainability in terms of quantitative values associated with ecology and performance, others emphasise qualitative factors, including socio-political issues. The great struggle operating within this context is the conflict of ecology and economy with creativity, and of creativity with instrumentality. How do we address the incompatibility of market-driven urban expansion, natural factors and the protection of a society's heritage? And what is the role of the designer in the development of urban design? More importantly, how can ideas be communicated and represented in a manner that facilitates discussion between all the parties involved?

For three years, from 2005 to 2008, AA Diploma Unit 14 was a testing ground for the creation of *mediating instruments*, installations that politicised consultation, communication and design strategies for developments in the Thames Gateway, as well as pursuing a range of design objectives. This essay will concentrate on the case study of a design proposal for the expansion of the East London Green Grid, a 'network' of public green spaces. It will show how mediating processes, together with the analysis of both quantitative and qualitative factors, can affect the design of alternative suburban topographies, allowing different forms of habitation. Such landscapes, reflecting both public engagement and a consideration of ecological factors, would have the potential to be highly versatile, encouraging rather than suppressing a variety of uses.

In an exhibition at the AA in London called 'The Thames Gateway Assembly', the unit tried to address the dilemmas faced by architects in the context of its ongoing research into London's expansion of the Thames Gateway. The exhibition showcased a series of mediating instruments that combined various aspects of sustainable planning. The most successful provided a platform for effective discussion between socio-political and environmental bodies. Some of the questions raised during these discussions are summarised by Lawrence Barth:

> How might architects apply themselves to the future of the Thames Gateway? Its vastness seems poorly matched with the usual scale of an architect's attention. In the popular mind, an architect is trained to design houses, or maybe the odd museum, office tower, or library. Assigned to the 80,000 hectares of the Thames Gateway, one might imagine, the architect simply begins to project these once-discreet objects in massive numbers across a landscape. The visualisation may suggest the potential of transformation, but it typically remains static, vaguely utopian and quickly forgotten. What if, instead, architects used their training to create interactive media to show how urban and environmental systems might work over time? What if they developed instruments which encouraged people to form assemblies around the consideration of the large-scale functional systems driving urban development around them?[1]

1.   Lawrence Barth, 'The Thames Gateway
Assembly' in *AA Files* 54 (2006), 67.

The discussion centred around the proposal outlined in the London Plan by the Mayor of London in 2004[2] for the construction of 120,000 new suburban homes and the necessary infrastructures in the Thames Estuary over the next ten years. Most of these new-build communities and cities will be riverside developments, built on current flood plains and brown fields. Given the capacity of London's existing flood defences, these developments pose an immediate conflict between nature and society. Although there are proven examples of successful flood mitigation systems in the Netherlands, which take into account the relevant natural factors, the demands of London's overheated property market deems such solutions unviable. Developers are looking for the 'New York Central Park Effect', in which the vicinity to 'nature' boosts both demand and prices.[3]

One component of the flood risk management has been the introduction of the East London Green Grid. Described by the Thames Gateway London Partnership as 'a living network of parks, green spaces, river and other corridors connecting urban areas to the river Thames, the green belt and beyond',[4] its aim is to create a better environment for development. It is intended both to enhance biodiversity and other aspects of the area's ecology and to provide strategic public areas for local communities. Theoretically, in case of flooding, these strategically situated areas would serve as drainage basins and protect the surrounding developments. On paper it appears as the perfect solution to the eco-economic problems outlined above. Unfortunately, the speed of ongoing developments, together with the lack of funds and the multiplicity of agents involved in the planning process, makes it very difficult for the Green Grid to be implemented in parallel with ongoing developments.[5] In order to understand how cultural, social, political and economic considerations can be reconciled with the conditions of the natural world, it is vital to create a dynamic relationship between these different factors. As James Corner put it, 'the promise of landscape urbanism is the development of a space-time ecology that treats all forces and agents working in the urban field and considers them as continuous networks of inter-relationships.'[6]

Networks of planners, environmentalists and local communities are often unable to communicate effectively. Despite the fact that most planning documents claim that local communities were consulted and that the design was derived from a bottom-up process, the unit's investigation into the planning of several projects in the Thames Gateway has proven quite the opposite. A large percentage of the local population was totally unaware of planned developments on their doorstep. New infrastructures and housing proposals in the Thames Gateway are mostly presented and discussed through the form of large-scale masterplans or maps. This form of representation, a tool of architects and urban planners, is not only unfamiliar to those outside of these professions, but also allows for distortion of information.

> Architecture's relationship with its representations is peculiar, powerful and absolutely critical. Architecture is driven by belief in the nature of the real and the physical: the specific qualities of one thing – its material, form, arrangement, substance, detail – over another. It is absolutely rooted in the idea of 'the thing itself'. Yet it is discussed, illustrated, explained – even defined – almost entirely through its representations.[7]

2. *The London Plan* (GLA, February 2004) available at www.london.gov.uk/thelondonplan/

3. 'A most canonical instance of this, of course, is Olmsted's Central Park, intended as relief from the relentless urban fabric of Manhattan – even though the catalytic effect that Central Park exerted on surrounding real estate development links it more closely with a landscape urbanist model. In this instance, landscape drives the process of city formation.' James Corner, 'Terra Fluxus' in Charles Waldheim (ed), *The Landscape Urbanism Reader* (New York: Princeton Architectural Press 2006), 21.

4. www.thames-gateway.org.uk/projects-content.asp?id=160

5. For detailed information see: *London under threat? Flooding risks in the Thames Gateway* (GLA, October 2005)

6. Corner, op cit note 3, 30.

7. Kester Rattenbury, 'This is not Architecture' in *Media Constructions* (London: Routledge 2002), xxi.

A case study in the form of a project by recent Diploma 14 graduate and AA Diploma Honours winner Richa Mukhia will help address these questions and suggest some conclusions.

'Propagating a Green Corridor' is a project that deals directly with the Green Grid and its relationship with the urban fabric, local communities and the developers' economic and political interests. Richa succeeded in making the issue a matter of public debate, creating a platform for discussion on a variety of levels, from intelligent interactive prototypes (as exhibited at the Architectural Association) to local initiatives and actions, from design manuals to inclusion in a government publication.

Instead of interpreting the Green Grid as a series of dispersed public green spaces, Richa's approach uses a green linking strategy as a form of negotiation tool between relevant parties. The urban fabric between the 'network' of parks is seen not as an interruption to this means of connection but rather as the playground for a grassroots initiative. The links, which Richa describes as 'Green Corridors', can begin to redefine the streetscape so that it is not merely seen as a territory for pedestrian and traffic flow but as a valuable public space in its own right. In addition, they can accommodate biodiverse habitats, pollution buffers and high-quality urban spaces.

In order to achieve these goals, it is important to recognise the public as experts in the territory that they inhabit and to integrate them into the planning process right from the outset. The issue of the Green Grid was made public through a series of guerrilla interventions, including the placing of patches of turf on the pavement or street markings on grass pitches, creating platforms of discussion not in a distant community hall but directly onto the sites on which the scheme would be implemented. Unlike conventional maps and diagrams of urban proposals, this strategy of representation avoids desocialisation of the territory affected. [8] The information, opinions and concerns were publicly documented in brochures, presentations and on a website.

Since some developments will not be constructed for another ten years, it seems essential to involve young people at an early stage, so as to increase their awareness of the dialogue concerning these issues. During workshops at local schools, the results of actual public consultations were discussed and the students were encouraged to voice their opinions using means of expression with which they were familiar.

This led to a second phase, in which proposals for a green corridor were displayed at the Architectural Association through an interactive device. The visitors were mainly people who are interested in the topic or are actually involved in some of the ongoing projects in the Thames Gateway. They were able to retrieve information and give informed opinions, which in turn were logged by the device. By shifting a variety of features related to the Green Corridors into position, every visitor could create his/her own preferred streetscape. A camera would detect any movement of these sliding elements and log this information, and an image on the screen would immediately display the visitors' evolving design. Over four weeks, significant data were received, directly influencing the design. In addition, on a less technological level, flower seeds were given away for people to plant in their front garden as the start of a branding campaign for the project. This combination of guerrilla gardening initiatives and applied academic research was the basis for a common representational language that proved to be appreciated by all the parties involved.

In a final step, the project identified three sites as testing grounds for green corridors. Through a series of drawings and animations as well as physical models with plants, possible transformations and growth over time were displayed. Together with a

8. As JB Harley notes, 'Maps as an impersonal type of knowledge tend to "desocialise" the territory they represent. They foster the notion of a socially empty space'; see 'Maps, Knowledge, and Power' in Denis Cosgrove and Stephen Daniels (eds), *The Iconography of Landscape* (Cambridge: CUP, 1988), 303.

design manual explaining in detail how to 'construct' public green corridors, this formed the basis of a design proposal ready to be implemented at any time.

This project was very successful in communicating strong design intentions to a variety of parties such as local communities, governmental and environmental bodies, as well as architects. Most significantly, as a result, the project has recently been included in a primer[9] issued by the Mayor of London and therefore makes strong claims to be implemented in the form of a planning policy. The Greater London Authority (GLA) has expressed keen interest in pursuing this method of engagement and is currently in conversation with Richa to realise some of the findings, methods and ideas associated with 'Propagating a Green Corridor'. This collaboration has fostered a highly valuable relationship between AA Diploma Unit 14 and the GLA, which will continue to effect change in London's landscape urbanism.

Turning to the particular agenda of AA Diploma Unit 14, we have reached the conclusion that the role of the architect has changed. Designing within the Thames Gateway requires mediation. This involves intelligent designs for the representation of proposals that are accessible to everyone affected. It also means independently informing relevant parties before receiving informed opinions. In turn, this demands a variety of communicative tools and platforms of discussion, such as the ones outlined in the case study above. The research of AA Diploma Unit 14 has proven that this can be a successful way to achieve higher levels of information transparency and engagement of all parties involved, forming a creative link between academia and practice.

9. Richa Mukhia's essay 'Green Grid as Social Network', co-written with AA Diploma Unit staff member Neil Davidson, was included in the 2006 GLA publication, *East London Green Grid Primer/ Eight Essays*.

Richa Mukhia, propagating a Green Corridor: 'interruptions' – a series of installations promoting awareness and discussion

'Interruptions': keep off the grass

'Interruptions': croquet

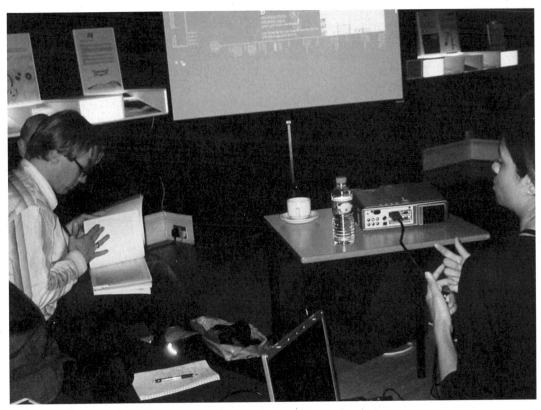

Richa Mukhia's presentation for the GLA in the Thames Gateway Assembly exhibition

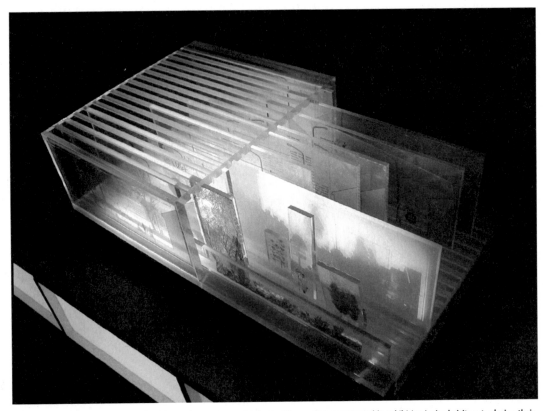

Richa Mukhia, propagating a Green Corridor: an interactive model for the Thames Gateway Assembly exhibition invited visitors to design their personal streetscape and digitally log the results

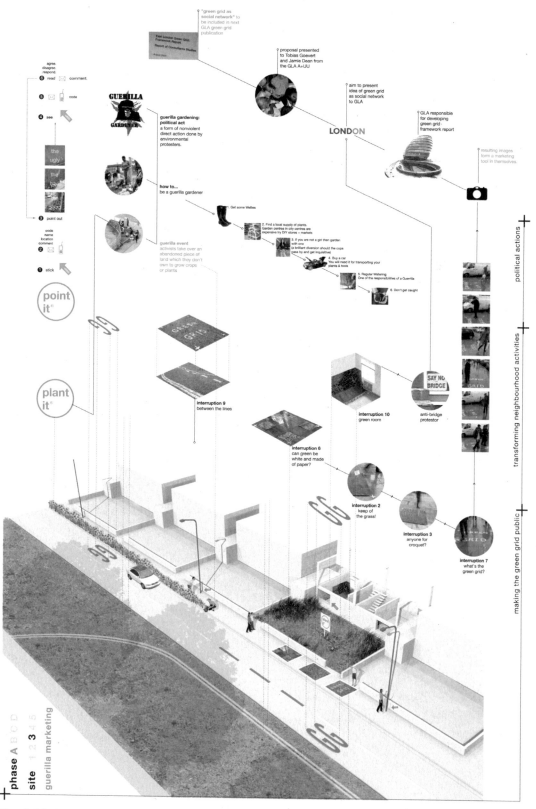

agree.
disagree.
respond.

6 read ✉ comment

5 ✉ 📱 code

4 see

the
ugly

the
bad

3 point out

code
name
location
comment

2 ✉ 📱

1 stick

point it®

plant it®

GUERILLA
GARDENER

guerilla gardening:
political act
a form of nonviolent
direct action done by
environmental
protesters.

how to...
be a guerilla gardener

guerilla event
activists take over an
abandoned piece of
land which they don't
own to grow crops
or plants

"green grid as
social network" to
be included in next
GLA green grid
publication

East London Green Grid:
Framework Report
Report of Consultants Studies
August 2005

proposal presented
to Tobias Goevert
and Jamie Dean from
the GLA A+UU

aim to present
idea of green grid
as social network
to GLA

GLA responsible
for developing
green grid
framework report

resulting images
form a marketing
tool in themselves.

LONDON

1. Get some Wellies

2. Find a local supply of plants.
Garden centres in city centres are
expensive to DIY stores + markets

3. If you are not a girl then garden
with one
(a brilliant diversion should the cops
pass by and get inquisitive)

4. Buy a car
You will need it for transporting your
plants & tools

5. Regular Watering
One of the responsibilities of a Guerilla

6. Don't get caught

interruption 9
between the lines

interruption 6
can green be
white and made
of paper?

interruption 10
green room

SAY NO
BRIDGE

anti-bridge
protestor

interruption 2
keep of
the grass!

interruption 3
anyone for
croquet?

interruption 7
what's the
green grid?

political actions

transforming neighbourhood activities

making the green grid public

phase A B C D

site 1 2 3 4 5

guerilla marketing

Phase 1 of the Green Corridor

37

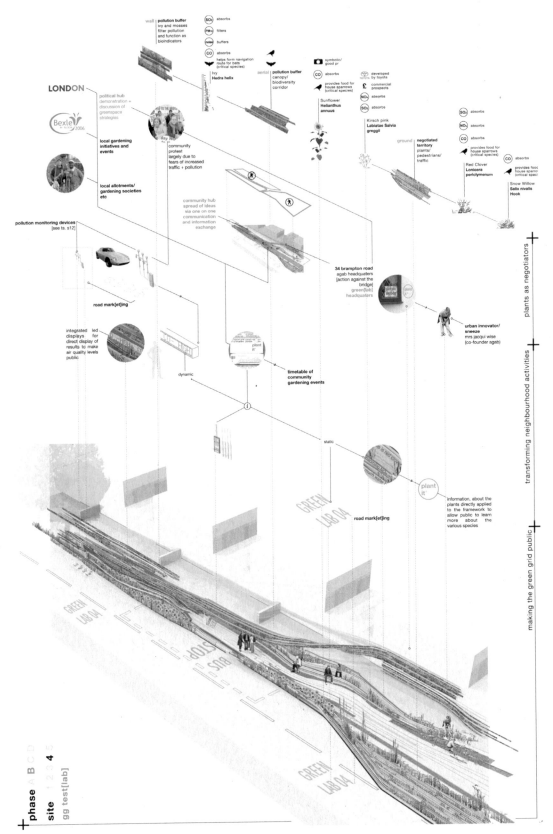

wall | pollution buffer
ivy and mosses
filter pollution
and function as
bioindicators

SO₂ absorbs
PM₁₀ filters
NOx buffers
CO absorbs
helps form navigation
route for bats
(critical species)

Ivy
Hedra helix

aerial | pollution buffer
canopy/
biodiversity
corridor

symbolic/
good pr
CO absorbs
provides food for
house sparrows
(critical species)

developed
by toyota
£ commercial
prospects
NOx absorbs
SO₂ absorbs

Sunflower
Helianthus
annuus

Kirsch pink
Labiatae Salvia
greggii

SO₂ absorbs
NOx absorbs
CO absorbs
provides food for
house sparrows
(critical species)
CO absorbs
provides food
house sparrow
(critical speci

LONDON

political hub
demonstration +
discussion of
greenspace
strategies

ground | negotiated
territory
plants/
pedestrians/
traffic

Red Clover
Lonicera
periclymenum

Snow Willow
Salix nivalis
Hook

Bexley
2006

local gardening
initiatives and
events

community
protest
largely due to
fears of increased
traffic + pollution

local allotments/
gardening societies
etc

community hub
spread of ideas
via one on one
communication
and information
exchange

pollution monitoring devices
[see ts. s12]

road mark[et]ing

34 brampton road
agab headquaters
[action against the
bridge]
green[lab]
headquaters

integrated led
displays for
direct display of
results to make
air quality levels
public

urban innovator/
sneeze
mrs jacqui wise
(co-founder agab)

dynamic

timetable of
community
gardening events

plants as negotiators

transforming neighbourhood activities

static

plant
it

information, about the
plants directly applied
to the framework to
allow public to learn
more about the
various species

road mark[et]ing

making the green grid public

GREEN
LAB 04

GREEN
LAB 04

BUS
STOP

GREEN
LAB 04

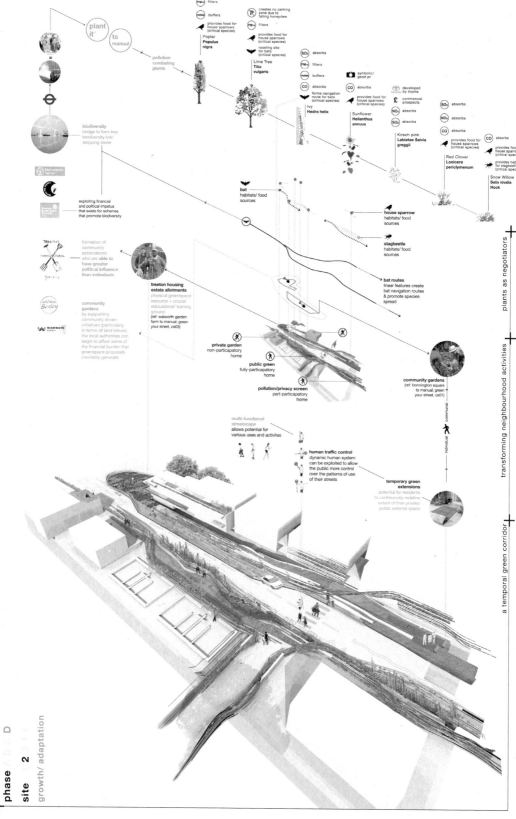

Phase 3 of the Green Corridor

Networks, Settlements and the Parliament of Architecture

Networks, Settlements and the Parliament of Architecture

Theo Lorenz

A design method can rarely be summarised in terms of a few 'products' or easy to understand statements. Examples of applied work are necessary to grasp its full significance. Even then, the task seems overwhelming, especially if you deal with a wide range of projects, as we did in the work of the unit. As a way of testing the method of mediated architecture we applied our work at three different scales: urban networks, settlements and the 'parliament of architecture'.

In order to provide a basis for our applied research, we worked for three consecutive years within the London Thames Gateway Development, the largest urban development in Europe, covering an area of over 80,000 hectares, from the Lea Valley to the Thames Estuary. The London Thames Gateway does not describe a clearly definable region but is rather a political term referring to vastly differing areas. These range from the urban fabric of London, with its dense population and developed infrastructure, to post-industrial brown-field sites and rural and coastal areas, with villages and small towns. It includes both sides of the River Thames, with Essex in the north, and Kent to the south.

One might expect this kind of political initiative – which treats widely diverse localities as if they comprise a unified area – would only create problems: it could be seen as London 'colonising' outlying areas through house-building. However, we were able to discover a deep well of opportunities, both to study projects that are already in delivery phase, and to tease out potential developments within the overarching political framework. In this context we could test the concepts of networks and mediation both as spectators and as active participants within the overall project. Students were given the opportunity to work within existing professional settings in an applied manner whilst challenging aspects of the scheme with innovative concepts and methodology.

Over the years many different institutions, organisations and practices have worked on the London Thames Gateway, in most cases focusing on very specific areas or projects. The work of AA Diploma 14, however, used the overall political situation of the Gateway as a testing ground for architectural negotiations and as a motor of design. We engaged with social, political, economic and ecological topics in a variety of combinations. The 'top-down' politics of the London Thames Gateway was challenged by various 'bottom-up' initiatives involving local interest groups and schools. The existing social networks, which were obviously challenged by the rapidly changing environment, were seen as offering an opportunity to create new connections. The project attempted to encourage and extend these networks, which were also seen as factors determining the design.

Environmental issues such as flooding, and the presence of both wildlife and contaminated brown-fields, invited the students to develop solutions that allow for a continued coexistence of flora, fauna and human habitation, as well as extending natural habitats into urban areas. Many projects tested possibilities of alternative economic models for the region and the new developments, often in combination with solutions to environmental and social issues. While the first year concentrated on research into the influence of the new Thames Gateway Bridge on the region's existing networks, the second year looked at the politically controversial approach to building 12,000 projected new homes in the Gateway. The third year focused on the potential for individual architectural projects to serve as agents for development and thus as 'parliaments of architecture'.

Nets at work

There are many examples of huge infrastructural projects throughout the world that are implemented within existing urban settings, following an overall strategy but hardly ever considering the repercussions of these new powerful *actants* on existing networks and systems. One of these projects is the highly disputed Thames Gateway Bridge, which was then the subject of a public inquiry. The 600-metre bridge linking Beckton (Newham) and Thamesmead (Greenwich) offered itself as an ideal study ground for the negotiation of architecture.

Our research concentrated on the political, social and physical influences of this proposed project on existing networks. As a linking structure the bridge re-engages both banks of the River Thames and the river itself. The unit worked with the implications of this new link for multiple levels of the urban fabric, as well as for landscape infrastructure. We tested how these strategies could influence planning and improve the design of the bridge itself. The student projects tested the possibility of using and reappropriating the bridge both during the creative process and through realisations arising from existing and new networks. In this way the bridge could be used as a generator for new projects, rather than an isolated, 'indisputable fact' that can either be accepted or denied. Because of this approach, some of the unit's initiatives and ideas remain relevant and active, even though the bridge itself has now been put indefinitely on hold.

A series of projects used the mediations occurring between human and non-human participants and inserted new *actants* into the process. These varied from human activities to technical experiments and in most cases were a combination of both. To achieve this objective the students worked throughout the year both on individual projects and on group installations. As an initial focal point of discussion we set up a four-week collaborative project entitled 'architects in residence', using four interactive installations to initiate discussions and mediations regarding the political, social and economic discourses. It was from these discussions and ideas that the students developed their individual theses.

The various projects exploited the potential of the bridge project, often by addressing its apparent conflicts and repercussions, from the long building process to the obvious increase in traffic, and the issues surrounding its environmental impact on the river. These controversies inspired a variety of stimulating proposals such as Richa Mukhia's Green Grid extension, Alex Thomas's local business and education programmes proposed for the duration of the construction phase, and Max Babbe's transformation of the bridge approach into a local information system. These proposals not only revealed the positive side effects of an otherwise problematic development, but actually started to influence the overall project itself, opening up discussions with the region's planning organisations. The experience showed that even if projects are already in place they can be reformulated into positive regeneration tools, rather than being either just denied or passively accepted. An integration of architects and local communities can bring otherwise abstract policies into action through the reappropriation of large public projects.

AADip14 concluded the year's work with a month-long exhibition, 'Thames Gateway Assembly', at the AA Gallery. Here the students' work was discussed alongside 32 projects about the Thames Gateway from the last decade which had already been debated and publicised. The points under discussion ranged from environmental, political and social issues to the scheme's urban qualities, its architecture and infrastructure – topics that had rarely been considered before in this way, largely due to the complex network of projects involved. In addition to members of AADip14, architects, AA Council members and students associated with the Architectural Association participated in the display, bringing together for the first time an 'assembly of ideas' for the Thames Gateway rather than merely a politicised overview of the project.

At the heart of the exhibition was a six-metre-long interactive table: on one side visitors could explore the different projects in detail, and on the other side discuss the issues at hand by moving around virtual planning equipment. The results were logged and displayed at all times. Meanwhile, as an extension of the central table, interactive installations presented new approaches for the overall development, sparking a vibrant discussion within the AA School and the stakeholders of the Thames Gateway. The installations were designed as negotiation tools for the projects, each of which dealt with a different aspect of the Thames Gateway Project – infrastructure, ecology and economy, contamination and flooding – thus forming a network of expertise.

However, the most significant success of the exhibition was that the whole display became a working example of applied design, initiating new collaborations and encouraging an overall understanding of the otherwise abstract Thames Gateway Project. The exhibition was accompanied by several stimulating events, ranging from expert lectures and film events to discussions with Buro Happold and the Greater London Authority. These allowed the students not only to test and discuss their final projects with a wider audience, but also to extend the work beyond the requirements of academia into the broader realms of practice.

Settlements

Building on this experience of the reappropriation of policies and projects into actual design tools for negotiation, AADip14 went on to research the main governmental aim of new settlements in the Thames Gateway, exploring the notion of new 'political settlements' and how these might be achieved.

Metropolitan expansion is invading the London Thames Gateway with 120,000 new homes planned for the next decade. Ninety-one per cent of these riverside developments are situated on the flood plain, creating an immediate conflict between nature and society. The mechanisms for these developments appear largely ad hoc, with no overall strategy for the wider region. The appropriateness of creating large numbers of homes on a flood plain, the impact upon some of the UK's most significant peripheral landscapes and environments, and the economic/infrastructural feasibility of these proposals are only mentioned in hushed tones. The democratic forum for these discussions is neither obvious nor accessible.

While continuing to design and develop the Thames Gateway Assembly, we explored the creation of both political and actual settlements within the region. Consequently, the assembly and its prototypical form of representation became a crucial component of the project's design processes. Cultural, social, political and economic environments were understood as embedded in the 'natural' world, defining the networks of interrelations of all the forces and *actants* working on the development.

During a series of forums, symposia and installations, the following questions formed the basis of our discussions: What is the potential for such a diverse network to mediate between its different *actants*, and how does it form and transform over time? Can we empower such a collective to allow for a perpetual discourse whilst being able to implement sustainable solutions and facilitate decision-making? Most importantly, can we attain through such an assembly a design that delivers an enriched creative settlement?

The unit started the year with a design competition sponsored by Brompton Bicycles, a public jury and an open event. The challenge posed by the competition was to find a different form of settlement for the 2007 Tour de France stage in London. In other words, what temporary and permanent settlements could be generated along the route of the event? The students' responses offered a range of ideas and solutions, from suggestive design and discussion tools to environmental, security and economical installations and applied planning manuals. Early in the academic year the students had to develop methods of representation that would allow them to discuss their diverse proposals with a prominent jury, which included Tobias Goevert (GLA AUU), Lisa Mackenzie (ECA), Alex de Rijke (dRMM) and Andrew Ritchie (CEO and inventor of Brompton), as well as John Worthington (DEGW/ CABE).

The topic of 'settlements' generated a wide range of designed 'settlements' and participatory projects in the students' work. The solutions dealt with a variety of policies and design solutions, ranging from architect-managed but self-built communities, as in Levent Kerimol's project; to Mellis Haward's cycling strategy for the Thames Gateway through a collaboration with the new Crossrail network; strategic green gardening in Celina Martinez-Cañavate's project; Alex Thomas's proposal for a new material-based cohabitation of local flora and fauna within newly built settlements; Ekapob Suksudpaisarn's network-based urban design tools; and Nausica Gabrielide's 'logo house', a co-sponsored housing project. Again the unit tested the results of the research beyond the academic environment of the AA, with a public exhibition and presentation, entitled 'Guerilla Gateway', at the Kemistry Gallery in London.

During the course of the year, it became very apparent that a topic as large as 'settlements' can extend in two directions, either as straightforward design solutions or as interventions that aim to change strategy or policy. The line between both becomes fluid within the context of the work's extensive ambitions. However, the knowledge gained, and the range of ideas and solutions that were achieved revealed the full potential of the methodology of mediation within applied projects.

The Parliament of Architecture

In the third and final year of the Thames Gateway Project, AADip14 explored the potential for the design of a building as the starting point for negation and transformation. The year was subdivided into three stages – 'design', 'transform', and 'apply'.

We started immediately with the design of a 'building', a term-long competition for 'A Parliament for Architecture'. The buildings that the students designed were required to curate the accumulated knowledge and research concerning the Thames Gateway Development, and to offer possibilities for interaction and decision-making as part of the design. The students were asked to design a building that was able to represent the 'assembly of the Thames Gateway', embodying and representing the multifarious parties involved with and living in the area. By parties we meant not only people – politicians and citizens, architects and developers – but also the flora and fauna found in the Gateway's ecosystem. An important part of the competition proposal was either to choose from a spectrum of possible typologies for an 'assembly space', or to hybridise several existing forms in order to create a novel typological compound. The proposals ranged from 'amphibious theatres' and swimming mosques to waterborne hotels, green trading towers, recycling stations, water cleaning and filtering parks, transport systems, power stations and even a spa.

For the competition itself it was important that the modes of representation for the students' ideas should incorporate multiple aspects of the design in the space of a glance, whilst also managing to be overall 'designs' in themselves. All submitted works were paper-based hybrids of drawing and model-making, on a one-by-two-metre panel. To test the 'design quality' of the 'parliament', the jury was chosen as a multidisciplinary panel with Charles Tashima, an architect, Nina Power, a philosopher, Jonathan Laventhol, technology director of Imagination, and Christian Kuesters, a graphic designer. This offered the students a range of critics whom they could use to 'transform' and develop the initial design on different levels.

In Ben Burley's 'Trading Tower' project, this transformation of an initial idea, which functioned as a generator of solutions, was very striking. Ben proposed an epiphytic vertical landscape infrastructure, growing alongside a planned office tower in Canary Wharf. His project operates within the context of green stock and carbon trading, two rapid growth sectors in the financial markets. His initial formal suggestion of linking 'green' tubes was later developed into the concept of an envelope acting both as a facilitator for renewable energy exchange between high-rise buildings and as a mediator that visually manifested the processes of green stock exchanges. These processes were also architecturally embodied in the distribution of tubular algae culture production facilities on the facades of the towers. The resulting vertical landscape embeds a series of public spaces ranging from actual trading floors to assemblies and recreational parks.

The last stage for the now transformed projects was to test and 'apply' them, turning them from ideas into projects that would manifestly change conditions and actual networks within the Thames Gateway or comparable sites. How could the students' projects start to foster real discussion and negotiation and provide new solutions for policy? In Maciej's project, the Waterborne Place, floating parks and related facilities are used as part of the negotiation possibilities created by section 106 of the Town and Country Planning Act 1990. Maciej used his project and its representation to discuss and collaborate with the actual parties in the area, thus creating on multiple levels an effective and adaptable 'lobbying space'.

AADip14's three years of research and applied projects within the Thames Gateway revealed many examples of how to achieve actual design and solutions within a complex framework that often seems opaque and impossible to engage with. Most importantly, the students of AADip14 learned to negotiate and develop their ideas, enabling them to pursue successful and independent careers as continuously 'creative' designers.

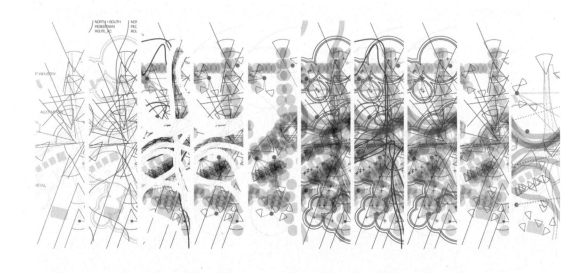

Max Babbe, reconfigured Thames Gateway Bridge, 2006

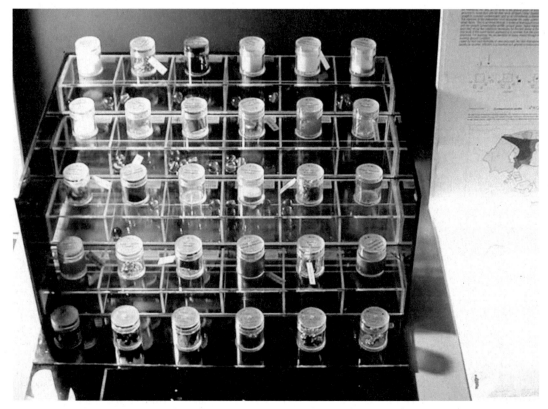

Abigail Tuttle, Tripcock Park decontamination, 2006

Alex Thomas, habitable concrete wall, 2007

Celina Martinez-Cañavate, productive scapes, 2007

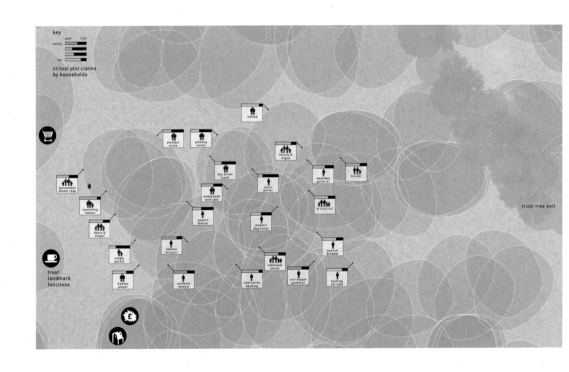

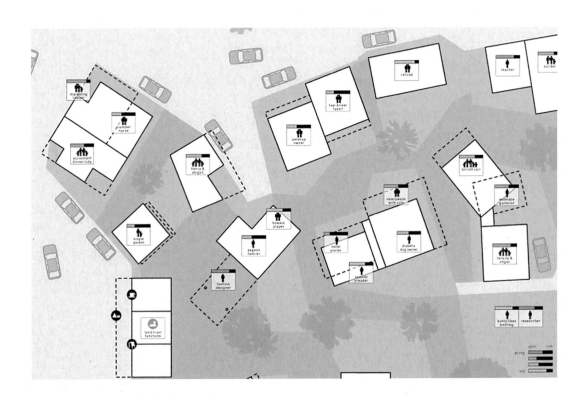

Levent Kerimol, self-build suburb, 2007

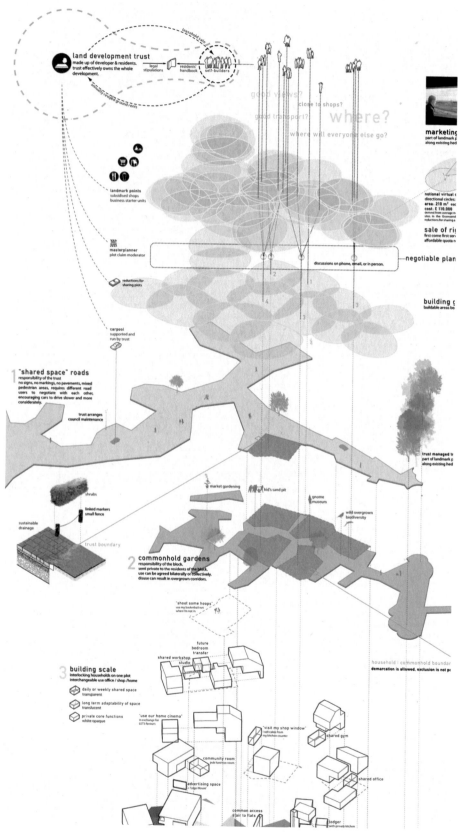

land development trust
made up of developer & residents.
trust effectively owns the whole
development.

legal stipulations
residents' handbook
self-builders

good views?
close to shops?
good transport?
where?
where will everyone else go?

marketing
part of landmark p
along existing hed

landmark points
subsidised shops
business starter units

national virtual c
directional circles:
area: 210 m² eac
cost: € 110.000
derived from average m
sites in the Greensand
reductions for sharing a

masterplanner
plot claim moderator

discussions on phone, email, or in person.

negotiable plan

reductions for
sharing plots

sale of ri
first come first serv
affordable quota n

building
buildable areas be

carpool
supported and
run by trust

1 "shared space" roads
responsibility of the trust
no signs, no markings, no pavements, mixed
pedestrian areas, requires different road
users to negotiate with each other,
encouraging cars to drive slower and more
considerately.

trust arranges
council maintenance

trust managed t
part of landmark p
along existing hed

market gardening
kid's sand pit
gnome museum

wild overgrown
biodiversity

shrubs

linked markers
small fence

sustainable
drainage

trust boundary

2 commonhold gardens
responsibility of the block.
semi private to the residents of the block.
use can be agreed bilaterally or collectively.
disuse can result in overgrown corridors.

"shoot some hoops"
use my basketball net
when I'm not in.

future
bedroom
transfer

shared workshop
studio

household | commonhold boundar
demarcation is allowed, exclusion is not po

3 building scale
interlocking households on one plot
interchangeable use office / shop /home

daily or weekly shared space
transparent

long term adaptability of space
translucent

private core functions
white opaque

"use our home cinema"
in exchange for
LETS favours

"visit my shop window"
I sell cakes from
my kitchen counter

shared gym

community room
pub function room

advertising space
a "Edge House"

shared office

common access
stair to flats

lodger
with private kitchen

Levent Kerimol, self-build development project, 2007

51

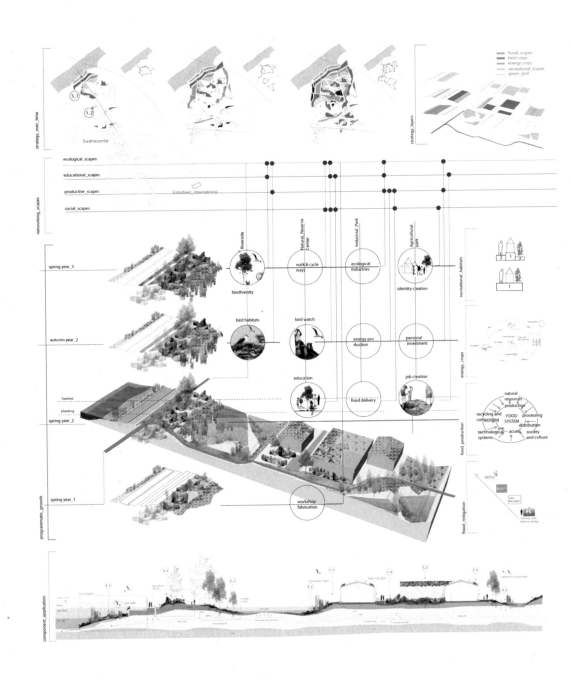

Symbiosis between two projects: Celina Martinez-Cañavate's productive scapes and Mellis Haward's cycle line, 2007

Mellis Haward, cycle line, 2007

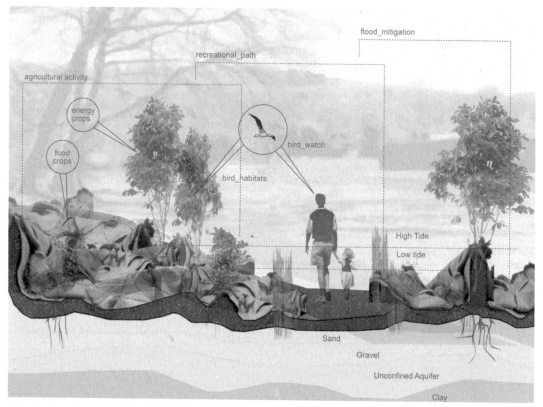

flood_mitigation

recreational_path

agricultural activity

energy crops

food crops

bird_watch

bird_habitats

High Tide

Low tide

Sand

Gravel

Unconfined Aquifer

Clay

Celina Martinez-Cañavate, productive scapes, 2007

[01] TITLE >	Energy Exchange Envelope
[02] DESCRIPTION >	Detail of Algae Growth Facade
[03] SCALE >	1:09

[14]

[Energy exchange envelope]

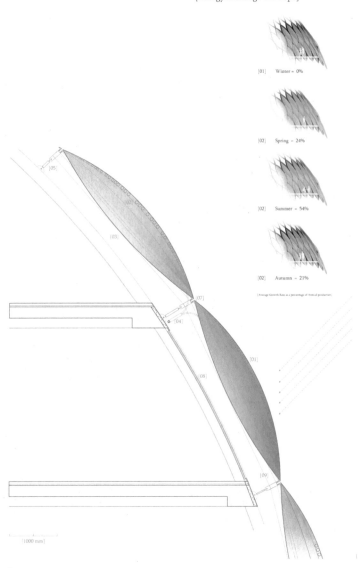

[01]   Winter = 0%

[02]   Spring = 24%

[02]   Summer = 54%

[02]   Autumn = 21%

[Average Growth Rate as a percentage of Annual production]

[1000 mm]

Section Through pneumatic ETFE Pillow

[01]   External pneumatic ETFE membrane carbon 0.25mm
[02]   Central ETFE 0.25mm membrane - Thermal reflective foil
[03]   Inner ETFE 0.25mm membrane
[04]   100mm dia - Air supply tube in pneumatic element
[05]   Tubular steel hinged column
[06]   760x460x mid on 180mm steel SHS
[07]   Polypropylene Algae growth tube
         (Length 25m, surface area 3 m2, Tube volume per cushion 0.045 m3)
[08]   Post and rail facade - double glazing unit
[09]   120/220 mm steel RHS
[10]   50 mm dia - Air supply tube in cushion - Internal Pressure 300 pa

General description

[01] This ETFE cushion incorporates a productive growth layer on the external facing membrane.

[02] From the ETFE water studies the tubular algae culture system has been employed as it provides the best weight to surface area ratio. This allowed the greatest productive

[03] The cushion develops a sandwich system of layered ETFE foil skin, polypropylene capillary tubes and a central theme reflective membrane to focus solar gains onto the growth tubes.

The Great Carbon Bazaar - London's green stock market
Ben Burley AA Dip 14 - Liquid Cities/Liquid Landscapes

Ben Burley, trading towers: seasonal facade system, 2008

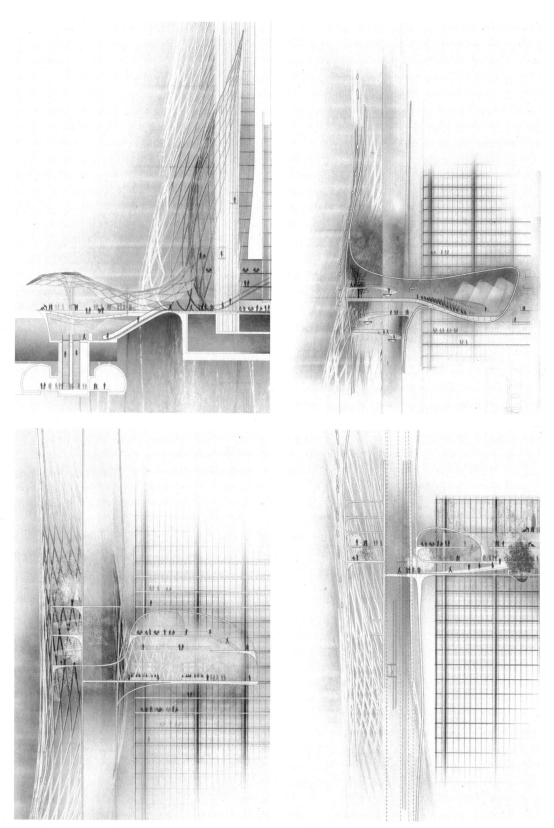

Ben Burley, trading towers, 2008

55

2D or not 2D
What's Lost in Translation Between the Dimensions?

2D or not 2D
What's Lost in Translation Between the Dimensions?

Peter Staub

For many architects, designing rather than building is the easier and often more enjoyable part of the profession. We all claim to be good designers and we probably all know how to represent architecture visually and spatially through a variety of techniques. We can build digital and analogue three-dimensional models, produce montages and collages, draw diagrams and scale-drawings and use any other media, ranging from 2D to 3D to time-based 4D and interactive 5D, to help communicate a project. Although that is a remarkable catalogue of skills in constantly evolving contemporary techniques and technologies, it becomes of secondary importance during the construction phase of a building. The building industry is slowly adapting to integrated design tools that allow multiple parties to collaborate using a common tool, but still relies principally on traditional methods of numerical representations, such as detailed construction drawings to scale. The creative design process still has to be translated into such a format. Built architecture is three dimensional, yet most abstracted information leading to it is two-dimensional. But what exactly is lost (or gained?) in this translation? What happens in between the 2D and the 3D?

Traditionally, design is a phased process, up to the point of construction. This process includes a range of techniques, from interpretative sketches and abstract spatial diagrams to scale drawings in 2D or 3D; from sketch models experimenting with massing and proportions to detailed models for presentation to the client; from digital three-dimensional models to photorealistic images, animated scenes and analogue outputs. It seems obvious that the techniques and technology used during the design process have a significant role in determining the built outcome. For example, key innovations in computer-aided design, manufacturing technologies and construction processes have enabled designers to explore beyond the right angle. Software can simulate any building in any condition, helping to eliminate risks that previously prohibited construction. However advantageous such innovations might be, they still do not change the designer's need to represent three-dimensional space through a series of vertical (sections) or horizontal (plans) cuts. Thus, although space may be conceived of in three dimensions, in the form of volumes and continuous, connecting surfaces, the information provided to those outside the discipline still consists of infinite and sequential two-dimensional layers. What if we were to invert this effect? Could we develop space (architecture) from two-dimensional information (representations of architecture) rather than the other way around? Could we find ways to bridge the gap between two and three dimensions by growing space out of the flat drawing?

As part of our investigation into representational techniques, our students were asked to experiment with what we describe as 2.5D – a spatial representation that does not have all the properties of either a drawing or a model, but consists of a combination of both. In traditional terms these representations are comparable to bas-reliefs in art. Based on a drawing on paper and through a process of cutting, folding and bending, a third dimension (Z) can slowly emerge from a flat surface (X,Y), which in turn transforms and distorts the original drawing below. This process, seen as a mediation between dimensions, often results in surprising outcomes. The depth of the newly created bas-relief, the Z axis, together with the effects of natural light and shadow, creates a visual experience of space. Furthermore, it requires the viewer to find specific viewing points from where perspectives of specific spaces should emerge.

It is interesting to observe that when the information in a two-dimensional drawing (for example, a section or a plan to a scale) is interpreted spatially, its embedded codes, such as its dimensions, hatching, colours and line weights, are misinterpreted or simply translated into space according to a different set of criteria and rules. This apparently random design methodology highlights the task of finding a common design language, a code that transfers spatial information between the dimensions. As in topographical maps, in which lines and their density correspond to a three-dimensional terrain, here the experiment is focusing on ways of interpreting the drawing of a building in order to extract its embedded topography.

So are we to conclude that architecture depends on codes? It appears to be fairly obvious that the tools we use during the design process to some extent predetermine the architecture. By tools I do not only mean quantitative software, although admittedly this plays a defining role in encouraging or discouraging a certain type of formal output, but I also include qualitative methods that lead to a multidimensional, atmospheric result.

I elaborated on the qualitative effects of two-dimensional layers in space in a project that was nominated in 2007 for the Swiss Art Award. This installation, entitled 'The 17th Man', is part of ongoing research into alternative ways to communicate architectural projects. The aim was to separate information about a project on a series of two-dimensional layers which, when laid over each other and illuminated from behind, would provide an atmospheric impression of the architecture.

'The 17th Man' is a floating spectator island specifically designed for the America's Cup sailing competition. Anchored just off shore, the floating viewing platform enables spectators to follow the boats during races as well as when they are in harbour. More importantly, the platform acts as a wave damper, absorbing the Mediterranean's wave energy and protecting Valencia's shore. The island offers the spectator the possibility to watch the boat races live and from close up, but also provides screen viewing, entertainment and hospitality.

There are three different types of spectator watching the America's Cup: some manage to see the races live on the water, others follow the event on big screens in the harbour development, while the bulk of fans view the regatta remotely from home on television or the internet. The aim of this project is to increase the interaction between all the spectators and the crews in a sport that was until now very difficult to experience. The floating spectator island introduces the mediated viewer as an additional design parameter defining the geometry of the structure. The built platform acts as a background embedded in the interface of the remote viewer. This means adapting the architecture to specific camera placements and movements in order to minimise its visual impact within the broadcast image. The outcome is an architecture that forms part of the event's choreography, blurring the boundaries of the virtual and real. Within the floating island's structural framework, pontoons not only enable the island to float but also provide controlled vertical movement corresponding to the sea's waves. The experience of being on water can, therefore, be transmitted directly to the spectator, helping to enhance the atmosphere of the event. If the pontoons are locked into place, a simple air pressure valve absorbs wave energy, making the structure entirely self-sufficient. The harvested energy can also be diverted to kinetic elements, such as screens and panels, which help to communicate the fans' support to the boats on the water.

The installation submitted for the Swiss Art Award consists of three oak boxes (640 x 280 x 480mm) with a flap opening the largest side. The three boxes are hung horizontally and adjacent to each other on the wall. Inside them are four Perspex layers, each at a distance of 20mm from each other and backlit by a neon light. In front of the installation, and connected to it by bent aluminium rods, are a series of transparent laser-cut postcard views. These provide precise viewpoints from where it is possible to observe specific information on the boxes' display layers. Each layer contains specific information: the outermost layer consists of text, the engraved foreground and vinyl cut elements acting as a graphic link to the layer behind. The middle layer contains the geometric build up of the structure according to the movement of cameras documenting the event: the geometry smoothly transforms from a plan view on the left into a sectional view on the right. The last layer, furthest into the box, is a print depicting the background of the floating island as well as additional numerical data. Each layer on its own is not really comprehensible, but as an ensemble and through a sense of depth this triptych offers an atmospheric reading of a complex project.

Designed as an exhibition piece, the installation also depends on the viewer's approach. Its aim is to convince at first glance, ensuring that the viewer approaches in search of further clues. On closer inspection, part of the text provides further insights and reveals the reasoning behind the abstracted geometries. Finally, if the viewer decides to go even closer, the detailed laser-edged foreground offers a further puzzle in the depiction of the architecture. Should this still not provide the necessary answers, three detailed booklets explain everything one wants to know about the floating spectator platform. In short, the communication strategy follows the concept: seduce – engage – inform. The atmospheric image and the overall composition must be intriguing, encouraging the viewer to know more. By discovering the requisite pieces in a puzzle of information, the viewer engages and feels in control. Finally, all the important information about the project must be made easily available. The level of detail increases towards the front of the installation, but is only visible when approaching closely. Since focusing on one layer is impossible, what dominates the human eye is the sense of depth, created by graphic overlaps on the parallel Perspex layers and appreciated only when the installation is seen in its entirety. In reality, the exaggerated third dimension is an optical trick, not too dissimilar to that of a stereo image.

Unlike the examples mentioned earlier, the installation for the '17th Man' explored an alternative reading of an already designed project. The installation did not help to design the architecture but was merely a visual machine of mediation, providing views and understandings of the project, which traditional plans, sections and other visualisations could not have offered. The effect created by the overlapping two-dimensional layers is that of a three-dimensional space, appearing much deeper than the actual installation – an increased visual depth, emerging from purely two-dimensional information.

There are a variety of ways to develop three-dimensional spaces out of two-dimensional data. Some of them can offer a pre-production design methodology, reinterpreting drawing codes and extracting surprising spatial results. In others, as in the example described above, it is not so much the real third dimension that is of interest but the three-dimensional effect created from the flat overlays. The results are often experimental, but when carefully composed, these installations can sometimes achieve effects that are impossible in either of the traditional techniques, 2D drawing or 3D model. The best results reveal something unexpected, which lies between the dimensions, without losing the atmospheric aspect of a model and the information contained in a drawing. So, there can actually be a significant gain, rather than a loss, from the exploration of the transition from two dimensions to three. Try it!

MAciej Woroniecki, Waterborne Place: panoramic view of the kinetic landscape

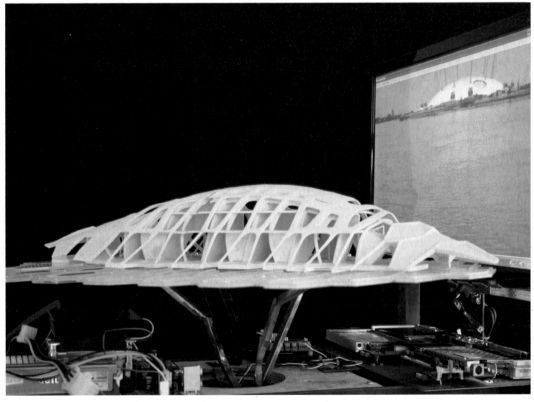

MAciej Woroniecki, Waterborne Place: 360-degree panorama at rest (above) and in motion (right)

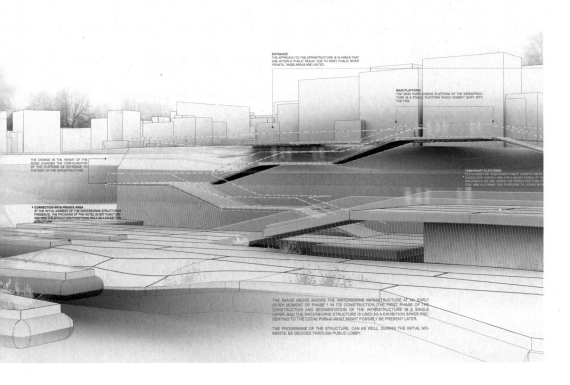

ENTRANCE
THE APPROACH TO THE INFRASTRUCTURE IS IN AREAS THAT
ARE WITHIN A PUBLIC REALM. DUE TO MANY PUBLIC RIVER
FRONTS, THESE AREAS ARE LIMITED.

MAIN PLATFORM
THE MAIN OVERLOOKING PLATFORM OF THE INFRASTRUC-
TURE IS A STABLE PLATFORM WHICH DOESN'T SHIFT WITH
THE TIDE.

THE CHANGE IN THE HEIGHT OF THE
RIVER CHANGES THE CONFIGURATION
OF THE PLATFORM AS ENTRANCE TO
THE REST OF THE INFRASTRUCTURE.

TEMPORARY PLATFORMS
PLATFORMS FOR TEMPORARY PUBLIC EVENTS CAN BE
DIDED VERY QUICKLY AND FOR A SHORT PERIOD OF TI
INFLATING A VOLUME UNDER THE INFRASTRUCTURE, AND
TIDE, AND ALLOWING THE PLATFORM TO LOWER WITH

• CONNECTION WITH PRIVATE AREA
AT THE INITIAL MOMENT OF THE WATERBORNE STRUCTURES
PRESENCE, THE PROGRAM OF THE HOTEL IS NOT FUNCTION-
ING AND THE STRUCTURE FUNCTIONS ONLY AS A EXHIBITION
STRUCTURE.

THE IMAGE ABOVE SHOWS THE WATERBORNE INFRASTRUCTURE AT AN EARLY
GIVEN MOMENT OF PHASE 1 IN ITS CONSTRUCTION. THE FIRST PHASE OF THE
CONSTRUCTION AND SEDIMENTATION OF THE INFRASTRUCTURE IS A SINGLE
LAYER, AND THE WATERBORNE STRUCTURE IS USED AS AN EXHIBITION SPACE PRE-
SENTING TO THE LOCAL PUBLIC WHAT MIGHT POSSIBLY BE PRESENT LATER.

THE PROGRAMME OF THE STRUCTURE, CAN AS WELL, DURING THE INITIAL MO-
MENTS, BE DECIDED THROUGH PUBLIC LOBBY.

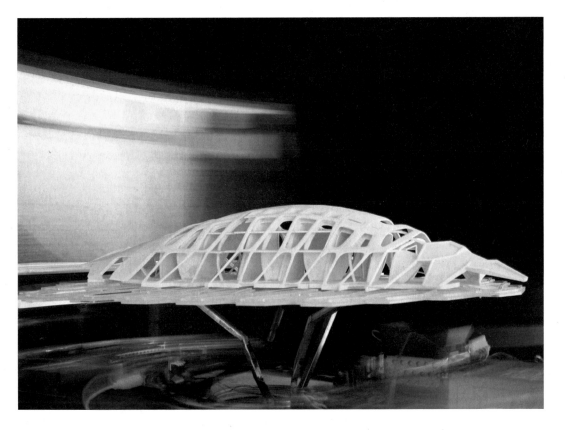

MAciej Woroniecki, Waterborne Place: projecting the settlement of floating structures along the Thames shore

Soo Jin, trading gateway: relief model

Dip14 installation in the AA end-of-year Projects Review exhibition

Francesca Rogers, harnessing waters

hydraulic panels, rotating using converted wave power

+1043.0

hydraulic panels, rotating using converted wave power

moving polyethylene pontoon in position +50 (max. elevation). air pressure valves are closed

stable positio and po Oscilla to gene

air pressure valves

+102.0 to +152.0

+102.0 to +152.0   +102.0

squa tube

Peter Staub, 17th Man installation, Swiss Art Award, 2007

Everything is not Necessarily Grey and Green

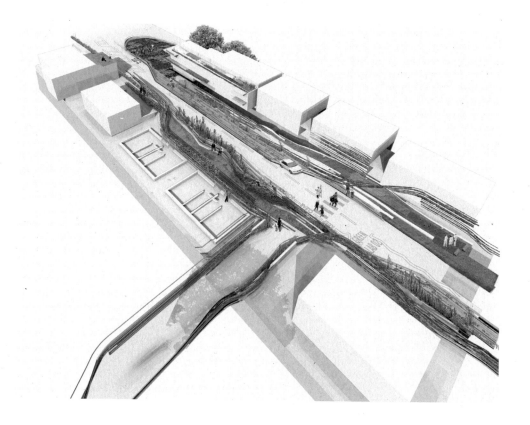

Everything is not Necessarily Grey and Green

Neil Davidson

Grey and green

When beginning an architectural project within the Thames Gateway, it is incorrect to assume that everything that is not grey is green. The Thames Gateway is a complex and challenging territory with hybridised conditions emerging from a combination of happy accident and generations of experimentation and reimaging designed to service the needs of the evolving metropolis. Pockets of contained wilderness sit comfortably on the edges of enormous areas of mass production; salt marshes and nature reserves occupy the shoreline of one of the busiest rivers in Europe, and brownfield sites rich in biodiversity and centuries of forgotten industrial heritage are developed by private and public sector investors in order to deliver fluctuating housing targets.

A conventional analysis of the landscape and built form of this part of London is inadequate. To adopt the popular approach to networked urban strategies – viewing the green and the urban spaces as distinct and mutually cancelling – limits both the imagination and the opportunities available. Most landscape strategies focus on improving the quality of existing green spaces rather than on developing physical links between them. A rethinking of this approach provides the opportunity to speculate, at both an academic and pragmatic level, on how a landscape infrastructure can contribute to the spaces between the 'network', viewing the intermediate urban fabric not as an 'interruption' to the rhythm of green space but as something integral to it.

The Diploma 14 student projects deliberately challenged this status quo and sought to harness the latent potential of the landscape, to make connections with the factors driving development in the Thames Gateway, whether political, social, cultural or economic, leading to the proliferation of new housing zones, transport corridors and eco-industrial parks.

Experts on the Thames Gateway

In parallel to the briefs set by the unit, the students developed and enhanced their own brief by becoming experts in the territory of the Thames Gateway. This was achieved on multiple levels:

- Through programmes of engagement with the people who live and work in the Thames Gateway
- Interaction with the agencies charged with delivering change, including the London Development Agency, Design for London and Transport for London
- Repeated exchange of ideas with developers and professionals working in the Thames Gateway
- Meeting experts in their chosen fields, from ecologists and project managers to hydrologists and manufacturers, initiating a knowledge transfer between academia and professionals.

At the beginning of each project, the location and connection of existing initiatives within the Thames Gateway was one of the most important elements of initial research, a catalyst for developing the brief. The methods employed during the collecting and cataloguing of the existing inputs and outputs of stakeholders within the region was as much a part of the design process as the final proposition. During this stage of project ideas, proposals, tools and techniques of representation were developed as a way of testing an applied approach to architectural design with the actual stakeholders of the Thames Gateway.

The most exciting solutions emerged when inventiveness was challenged by the requirements of necessity; and often when the magnitude of a landscape intervention occurred at an infrastructural scale while the effect was felt most acutely at the human scale. This was exemplified in Richa Mukhia's project, 'Green Grid as Social Network'.

The seed for this project was discovered by analysing the emerging landscape strategy of the East London Green Grid (Greater London Authority 2007) alongside the proposals for the Thames Gateway Bridge. The East London Green Grid was in the early stages of implementation and project definition: a handful of parks and public opens spaces had been created, regenerated and enhanced under the umbrella of the Green Grid. In parallel to this, proposals for the new bridge connecting Newham with Greenwich were being reviewed in a public enquiry. The implications of the new bridge across the Thames had far-reaching consequences, which were perceived mostly in positive terms at a regional level, and negatively at the local scale.

One of the methods advocated by this project was to recognise the public as experts – and quasi-clients – in their own domain. Advocacy of public involvement in the design and planning process defined a new role in which the public could become urban stewards with a personal interest at ground level. This theme was also picked up in the analysis and reinterpretation of the manifesto for Guerrilla Gardening by Celina Martinez-Cañavate and the explorations of Levent Kerimol of LETS (Local Exchange Trading Systems or Schemes) and the possibilities for applying them in the communities around Greenwich.

Each of these projects shared a common ambition to employ local green skills to influence city and landscape planning and to blur the boundaries between the grey and the green. The cultivation of community-driven greening initiatives on different scales would enable local communities to become active participants in the development of green space networks. This would provide the public with the tools for beginning to effect change and take ownership of their local environment. As a consequence, the task of 'Greening the Gateway' could be extended to the grassroots level, with community groups or even individuals propagating green corridors through simple actions.[1]

The availability of green skills is evident all across England in the form of the private garden. A precisely manicured plot next to the home is a much sought-after commodity, a pastime/obsession that is embedded in the national psyche. In a country of gardeners there are many people well equipped to cultivate, tend and maintain the landscapes of our cities. Green-fingered communities could contribute to the physical improvement of the urban environment as well as becoming important nodes for social exchange.

Unfortunately, a cursory look at many of the streets in the Thames Gateway quickly reveals that this is no gardener's idyll. Green verges have disappeared as roads have been widened, fences have replaced hedgerows, and efficient drainage has replaced the slow percolation of surface water into the surrounding landscape. Although the public landscapes are dynamic and complex, they do not form a picturesque construct or Royal Park and even in some cases the lush green of the front garden has given way to the grey desert of low-maintenance concrete pavers and a desirable private parking space.

It was clear, therefore, that the transfer of skills from the private garden to the public realm and the urban landscape could well be one of the biggest challenges to these initiatives. However, each project was clearly described with examples and evidence of how the proposals could be successfully developed to the next stage, making the transition from academia to reality.

1. Developed from an essay by Neil Davidson and Richa Mukhia in *The East London Green Grid Primer* (Greater London Authority, 2007).

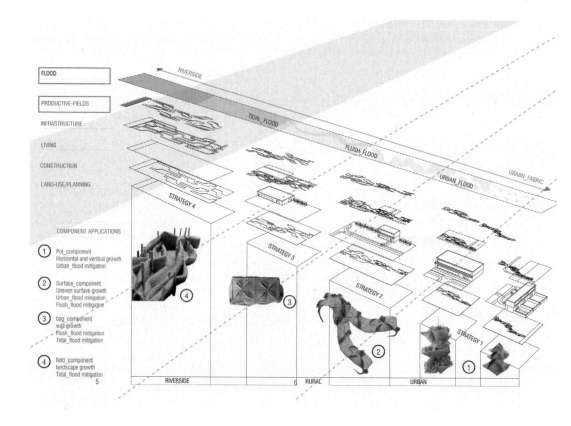

FLOOD

PRODUCTIVE-FIELDS

INFRASTRUCTURE

LIVING

CONSTRUCTION

LAND-USE/PLANNING

RIVERSIDE

TIDAL_FLOOD

FLUSH_FLOOD

URBAN_FLOOD

URABN_FABRIC

COMPONENT APPLICATIONS

(1) Pot_component
Horizontal and vertical growth
Urban_flood mitigation

(2) Surface_component
Uneven surfave growth
Urban_flood mitigation
Flush_flood mitigation

(3) bag_component
wall growth
Flush_flood mitigation
Tidal_flood mitigation

(4) field_component
landscape growth
Tidal_flood mitigation
5

STRATEGY 4

STRATEGY 3

STRATEGY 2

STRATEGY 1

RIVERSIDE   6   RURAL   URBAN

---

(1) Pot_component
Horizontal and vertical growth
Urban_flood mitigation

vertical_layout

horizontal_layout

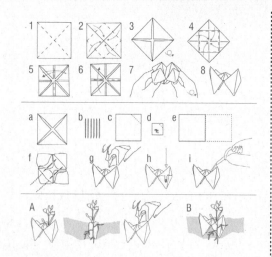

FOLDING- biodegradable jute patch 30 x 30cm

1 Fold side down on both diagonals and unfold

2 Fold all four corners to the center

3 Turn fabric over

4 Again fold all corners to the center

5 Fold fabric in half and unfold

6 Fold in half from top to botton. Do not unfold

7 Slide thumbs and forefingers under the squares and open the component

8 Turn over

CONTENT & APPLICATION

a 1 x unfolded component

b 6 x toothstick

c 1x soilbag

d 2 x seedbags: 1 x basil, 1 x lavender

e 1 x instructions

f perforate the component with 2 sticks as shown in illustration

g distribute soil in 4 equal parts

h place seed in the middle

i add water for moist soil and place where desired

GROWING & REPLANTING

A extract seedling and plant outside. Reuse the component

B For biodegration, plant whole component outside

MATERIALS

- biodegradable fabric; jute, hemp...
- biodegradable plastic
- wooden toothsticks
- recycled paper

Celina Martinez-Cañavate, productive scapes, 2007

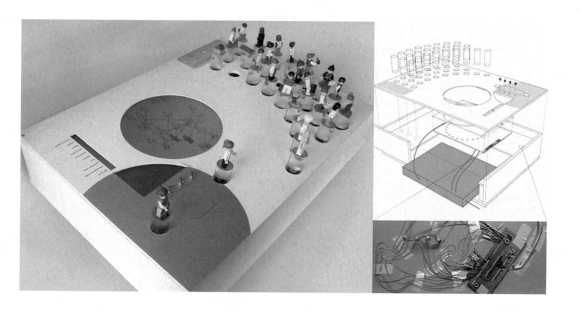

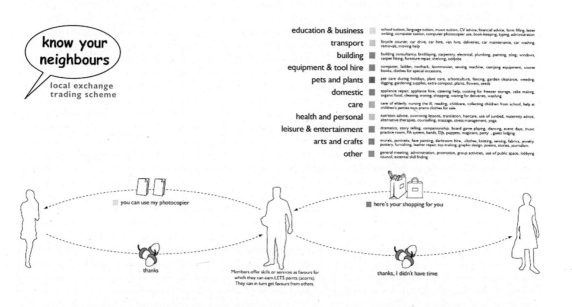

education & business	school tuition, language tuition, music tuition, CV advice, financial advice, form filling, letter writing, computer tuition, computer photocopier use, book-keeping, typing, administration
transport	bicycle courier, car drive, car hire, van hire, deliveries, car maintenance, car washing, removals, moving help
building	building consultancy, bricklaying, carpentry, electrical, plumbing, painting, tiling, windows, carpet fitting, furniture repair, shelving, oddjobs
equipment & tool hire	computer, ladder, roofrack, lawnmower, sewing machine, camping equipment, course books, clothes for special occasions
pets and plants	pet care during holidays, plant care, arboriculture, fencing, garden clearance, weeding, digging, gardening supplies, extra compost, plants, flowers, seeds
domestic	appliance repair, appliance hire, catering help, cooking for freezer storage, cake making, organic food, cleaning, ironing, shopping, waiting for deliveries, washing
care	care of elderly, nursing the ill, reading, childcare, collecting children from school, help at children's parties toys prams clothes for sale
health and personal	nutrition advice, swimming lessons, translation, haircare, use of sunbed, maternity advice, alternative therapies, counselling, massage, stress management, yoga
leisure & entertainment	dramatics, story telling, companionship, board game playing, dancing, event days, music practice rooms, PA system, bands, DJs, puppets, magicians, party , guest lodging
arts and crafts	murals, portraits, face painting, darkroom hire, clothes, knitting, sewing, fabrics, jewelry, pottery, furnishing, leather repair, toy making, graphic design, poems, stories, journalism
other	general meeting, administration, promotion, group activities, use of public space, lobbying council, external skill finding

Levent Kerimol, local exchange trading scheme, 2006

Mediating Urbanism

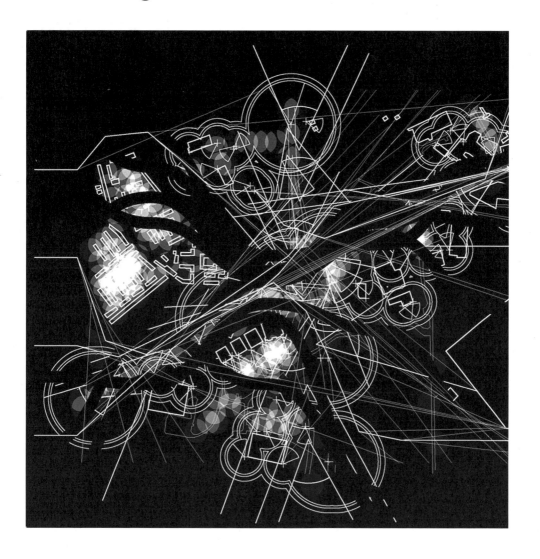

Mediating Urbanism

Tanja Siems

Architects and urban planners seem always to be on the search for the 'big idea', the unified 'vision' that would make our built environment better and more suited to its users' needs. Over the last few centuries we have seen various more or less clearly defined 'guiding principles' for spatial planning, which have shaped urban developments.

One of the most influential concepts was CIAM's 'Functional City', formulated as the Charter of Athens in 1933, which expressed the desire to make the city less concentrated, breaking it down into spatially divided areas with different functions (living, working, leisure and traffic). These principles were applied after World War II to urban structures through the policies of the 'organised' and the 'dispersed' city. In the 1960s and 1970s, the main guiding principles were 'urbanity through density', and the 'car-orientated city'. The consolidation and integration of the previously differentiated functional zones demanded by the Athens Charter, in combination with a dense population and complex infrastructural systems, achieved a kind of new urbanity in the city, but also produced sprawling suburban housing estates. In the 1980s and 1990s, following this decentralisation and suburbanisation of the urban structure, planning policies returned to intra-urban redevelopments and sustainable ecological planning.

But what principles exist today? At the moment, various urban policies such as 'polycentric decentralisation', 'in-between cities' and 'city of short distances' still aim to regulate the spatial and infrastructural growth of the city in order to from a stable network between the city and the region. In the last 15 years, the approach of urban space strategies has been to generate areas of predominantly mixed uses, densify the structure, and connect the heterogeneous environments of the city and region so as to reduce uncontrolled, monofunctional urban sprawl. Greening the city in order to counter carbon-dioxide emissions, lower ambient temperature, increase surface water retention and avoid flooding, are equally important as factors in the economic, environmental and social approaches to planning. However, urban and regional strength is also defined by social networks, including education, work, family, housing, community, health and safety, and it is of vital importance that these aspects are balanced within the urban condition, so as to provide an equal quality of life for everyone.

Planning policies guide the practice of planning and design without being legally binding, but they are an important means of representing and regulating future urban developments, and help to formulate time- and space-related strategies for the urban fabric. All stakeholders should be continually involved during the various phases of planning, in order to mediate and communicate the complex urban development processes and to provide a record of an integrated planning process. It is essential, therefore, to include non-hierarchical planning tools, procedures and instruments in the spatial development process. In this way the stakeholders become partners who are systematically and openly integrated into the resolution of planning decisions. Integrated planning does not generate rigid and inflexible scenarios, models, drawings or plans, but instead includes the elements of communication and organisation, with the aim of making them more adaptable and open to innovation.

Why develop urban policies and general principles, while focusing on frameworks and norms, if there are no strong guiding principles for spatial planning such as there were in the 1970s? In today's urban planning, it is less important to come up with new strategies or policies than to combine existing principles in order to reflect, reconfigure and preserve urban conditions. Cities still need a kind of attractive chaos of contrast and friction, and flexible, open but not fixed-use spaces in order to allow for future undefined developments. This principle of flexibility is very important for the urban fabric: it keeps areas free to develop over time, preserving incomplete spaces that can shift during the expansion of the city – spaces that will never be complete until they are inhabited.

Despite changing social environments and political situations, it appears that policies in recent urban developments are not new but rather variations of former strategies, such as the policies of 'urban density' and 'mixed use'. This marks a departure from the Charter of Athens principles, which produced mono-functional suburban city structures during the second half of the twentieth century. In order to revitalise cities in the 1990s, the new urban policies worked towards multi-functional, dense centres, returning to the prewar concept of the city. These urban developments show the importance of re-appropriating former strategies rather than defining new policies and guiding principles. Policies should be open and flexible, so as to adapt to any urban setting, and they should always mediate between the existing social, political and environmental urban conditions.

Mediation – a new urban policy?

If there is currently no new planning principle and most concepts have already been considered within earlier approaches, should we not see the adaptation of these principles to today's parameters and tools as our main objective instead of desperately searching for the new? It seems essential that we should concentrate on the mediation between all-important public and private stakeholders within an integrated planning process. The possibilities for this have been demonstrated by applied, mediated urban projects in Brussels and Ilford, as well as in certain case studies researched by AA students. The student projects indicate the importance of learning from existing norms, researching policies, and then implementing these strategies with actual designs, which are tested against various urban conditions. The testing of these defined spatial tools and the demonstration of the entire design process are as important as the final project, and form a significant part of the students' experience of learning from their failures and successes.

The students applied urban and infrastructural strategies to large-scale sites inside the Thames Gateway area, and also to cultivate a form of flexible overall development. Students' case studies used a range of diverse policies: the East London Green Grid Framework (Richa Mukhia's 'green grid applied at TGW Bridge'); the Biodiversity Action Plan (Ben Burley's 'trading tower'); the Section 106 agreement (MAciej Woroniecki's 'Waterborne Place'); the 'in-between cities'[1] strategy (Celina Martinez-Cañavate's 'productive scapes'); the 'conversion and mixed use' strategy to generate a 'city of short distances' (Mellis Haward's 'cycle line' and Max Babbe's 'information infrastructure'); and the 'decentralised concentration' guiding principle (Levent Kerimol's 'settlements – self-build suburbs'). The policies do not work in isolation within these projects but are intended to facilitate productive negotiation with the stakeholders.

An important method of applying new strategies to urban design is that of combination. If we could create a symbiosis between multiple interests and stakeholders, we might be able to realise projects that otherwise might not gain the required political or economic support. If we combine powerful or necessary projects and policies with many less powerful ones, we could achieve a more sustainable overall project that transforms all its initial premises.

One of these approaches is demonstrated by Mellis Haward's 'cycle line – green infrastructure'. This restructures the areas around an existing railway with simple, flexible pre-constructed elements which adapt to any existing situation on various sites. The new

1. Thomas Sieverts, *Zwischenstadt* (1997), English trans *Cities without Cities: An interpretation of the Zwischenstadt* (London: Spon Press, 2000).

structure interweaves mixed-use areas for housing, working, shopping and leisure with an infrastructural green network for pedestrians and cyclists. In London designated cycle routes, as functioning networks, often only exist on maps, and if actually present in the urban fabric, they are often not at all user-friendly. The problem lies with the funding of these routes, which are budgeted individually in the different boroughs and are therefore designed separately rather than as an overall network: often one cycle route is not linked to another, and ends in the middle of a busy street. How can cycle lanes be used as networks when the network is broken up and rendered illegible by the lack of communication between the different owners?

Mellis dealt with this problem by studying various urban and infrastructural policies, communal studies and frameworks, and talking to different planning departments at TfL (Transport for London) and the LDA (London Development Agency). Her solution was to use the Network Rail authority as a single landowner capable of providing the network system required by her infrastructural project. She used this opportunity to develop an alternative transport system that would provide a safe pedestrian, cycling and public transport route along one infrastructural network line. The mediation between existing policies, different planning institutions and the land-owner Network Rail allowed Mellis to develop her integrated green infrastructure route, which links the Thames Gateway area structurally and functionally with the centre of London. In this respect her concept of a reappropriated network system is a significant advance towards achieving a sustainable 'city of short distances'.

Another way in which a mediated design process can try to solve the problem of a scattered urban structure is through information networks. How can we distribute knowledge and information within the urban planning process? What systems might be re-appropriated in order to achieve an information exchange between users and planners? Max Babbe's project 'information infrastructure' proposes the re-assembly of infrastructure information technologies in order to create an active political space. By deploying infrastructure technologies at an early stage, and augmenting their existing outputs, the designer can extend their range of functions. With an interest in the ongoing public consultation process and the increasing presence of interactive technologies in our culture, this project attempts to make visible the space created by the use of measuring and viewing technologies.

An in-depth exploration of the re-use of these technologies resulted in an applied virtual and physical strategy. A virtual interface camera, for example, could produce dynamic suggestions for future urban developments, achieved by monitoring, in real-time, the use of spaces, after which surface infrastructure was designed according to the flow of people, density and usage. A physical strategy, applied through subtle land deformation, enables people to read the space as a series of politically active areas. These options were to be deployed in the urban fabric as tools to allow stakeholders to create their own, mediated environment in the marginal and underused areas around the Thames Gateway Bridge.

Alongside the combination of large-scale projects with existing infrastructures and technologies, it is also possible to use existing planning policies and somewhat 'dry' measures such as the section 106 agreement as motors of innovation. Section 106 deals with sustainable 'compensating measures' strategies: in most cases these are merely used to calculate the green and public spaces that must be provided in compensation for the losses caused by new developments. But how can this policy be used in dense urban areas in order to provide a sustainable environment through intelligent green systems?

In this context Ben Burley's project researches new ways of creating green facade planting systems. His vertical green infrastructure integrates specific algae in order to filter used and polluted air, and to produce oxygen in exchange. The facade structure is formed by ETFE cushions, which incorporate a productive growth layer on their external membrane. After different studies, the tubular algae culture system was employed in the project, as it provides the best weight-to-surface-area ratio, and this allowed the greatest level of oxygen production. The cushion develops a sandwich system of layered ETFE foil skin, polypropylene capillary tubes and a central reflective membrane in order to focus the sun's rays and maximise solar gain.

In comparison with Ben's vertical green system, MAciej Woroniecki's 'Floating Infrastructure' project is concerned with a sustainable green system on the eastern shore of the Isle of Dogs in the Thames tidal area. The project proposes the creation of an infrastructure that is negotiated through a public and private venture to produce public spaces. Here the Section 106 policy is used as the basis of an agreement concerning the project design proposal, which was the product of negotiation between all the stakeholders and relevant development partners. The project focuses on the process necessary to construct and adapt a floating pneumatic infrastructure facilitating new public programmes along the river. The environmental structure is negotiated during the development of the infrastructure. The production of a new physical public space pushes the project onto the next level, and gives a physical input to the community's environmental planning.

A practical approach: mediating between academia and practice

For our own practice it has always been very important to combine our teaching and our work in the office, and to link research to applied projects. These parallel activities have enabled us to support complex investigations within the unit framework, as well as to provide our clients with a broader testing ground for their projects. In order to maintain this cross-over between the professional and the academic, Dip14 acquired funding for projects and exhibitions from public and private institutions and bodies, from the LDA, who in 2004 sponsored the students' Crystal Palace park projects; Parkview International, who sponsored the students' research studies on Battersea Power station; and Brompton Bicycles and the LTGDC Corporation, who supported various Thames Gateway projects over two years.

All our urban, architectural and media projects are developed through an integrated planning process on all levels. Our urban development project in Brussels, an urban planning strategy with an integrated participatory pavilion, demonstrates this approach of mediation and re-appropriation during the planning process. From the start we integrated various private and public stakeholders in Brussels–Berchem, which is a complex, multi-cultural urban quarter in the northwest of Brussels. Within the broad local interest group, we involved people of different ages – from schoolchildren to elderly persons – and various cultural backgrounds in order to get a broader input concerning the different approaches that were possible and desirable for this public project.

Even as early as the competition tendering process, we interviewed various local people in order to get a general overview of the local situation. Furthermore, to make financially feasible an extensive and high-level urban environment – to be delivered through a high standard of design – we tried to combine different regional and local budgets in a creative way. An example of this was the reorganisation of architectural and art funds from the state and region in order to build a participatory pavilion, even before the whole urban and infrastructural project was to go on site. Rather than spending art funds for some monumental and unusable sculpture, this new participatory pavilion integrates various media systems in order to test different design ideas, bouncing them back from public to private stakeholders in a live dialogue that happens on site. This allows a real-time public consultation process during the different construction phases, and after completion the pavilion will accommodate public events and exhibitions in the new urban square.

During the two-year planning process for this complex urban and infrastructural project, we developed with the local architectural office B612 an integrated planning process which allowed us to generate a flexible urban design development that could adapt to private and public stakeholder suggestions at any time. From the first design studies up to the granting of planning permission, we arranged over 50 meetings with the region, the mayor, the district, TfL, the environmental office and the cyclist and pedestrian agency, plus eight major public consultation workshops with up to 300 people. During these workshops, we negotiated between the various requests made by participants and immediately integrated them into our design process. To handle this well, it was very important to act at the same time as a mediator and as a planner: only then could we be sure that the design was improved and enriched by the negotiations rather than losing all its important design details and core ideas.

The same method of using an integrated and open planning process was applied to our urban and landscape development project in Ilford, Greater London, for which JL Gibbons, in collaboration with t-2 Spatialwork, were selected after a long tendering process. Ilford is located in the Borough of Redbridge in the Thames Gateway development area. The communities in this area are even more segregated, and culturally diverse, than in the urban Berchem district of Brussels. Before we started with our framework strategy study, most of the areas had become run-down, with various gangs occupying the few existing open public spaces. To keep everyone involved during the planning and working process of our masterplan framework, it was very important to foster input from all the diverse local communities. Our consultation partner 'urban canda' started with direct interviewing sessions at the different site areas in Ilford, which were followed up by the design team's workshops with people from the various local communities.

The concept on which our framework was based combined the functions of living, working and leisure, so as to attract a mixed development to the neglected quarters alongside the river Roding. Our intention was that all projects should have a positive ripple effect on their adjacent areas, acting as a kind of catalyst for the whole urban region. To frame and connect these different project areas, we designed an overall structural timber boardwalk system along the shore of the river Roding. Our framework approach is different to that of a traditional masterplan study, as it relies on a more dynamic interpretation and understanding of the qualities and opportunities embedded within the different sites. Within two years of the completion of the Uphall park project and the Bridge installation, various groups from the local community had already begun using these two urban spaces in different ways. To apply the flexible design approach of our masterplan strategy over the next 25 years, the successes achieved by each realised project will need to react to future economic and ecological situations, so that future developments can be progressively implemented and integrated into the existing urban fabric.

'Mediative urbanism' negotiates and forms the interface between the form of cities and the needs and desires of their *actants*. In this context, the role of the mediator between all the relevant urban actors is vital for the realisation of an integrated and communicative planning process in which equal negotiation exists between all participating stakeholders, a synthesis of their demands into a holistic and fluid design process.

To reappropriate various urban strategies and to manage creatively the mediation between the planners, the authority, the public and the urban condition should always be the main concern for an integrated urban development. This integrative process requires cooperation between all planning actors – a cooperation at whose heart lies a flexible interdisciplinary approach, with the aim of sustainably transforming our complex urban fabrics. During the whole process, all important areas of planning practice and related activities will be connected, with the role of the public being to provide a continuously refreshed mandate, driving the design process onwards and invigorating these integrated planning operations. Spatial policies are assemblies of urban *actants*, providing ideals that will shape future developments and creating a foundation for strategic positions that will produce concrete results. By involving media, communication, research, design and conflict management tools, the planners should always be inventive, responsive and reactive to diverse and complex urban situations.

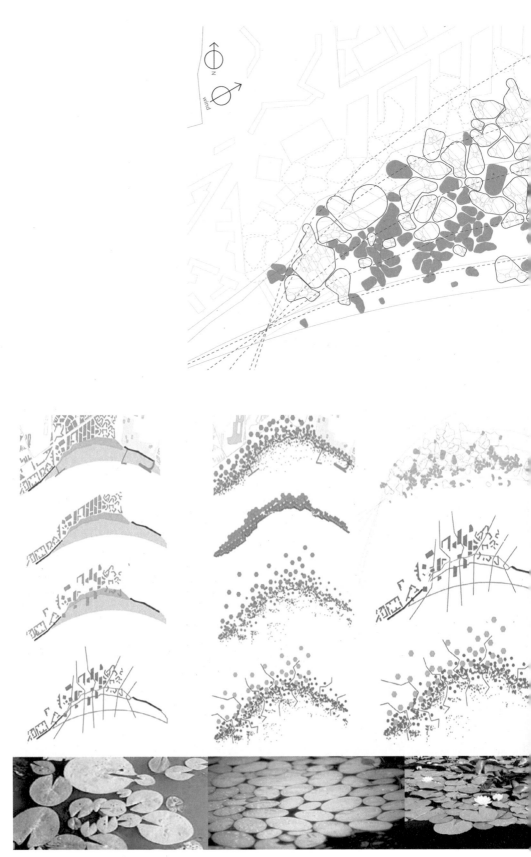

Celina Martinez-Cañavate, green masterplanning

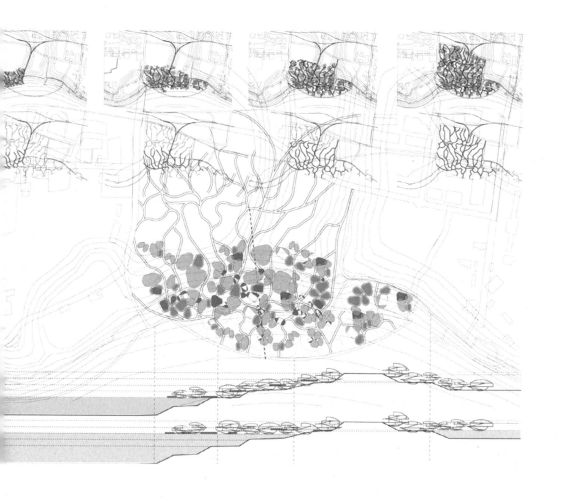

83

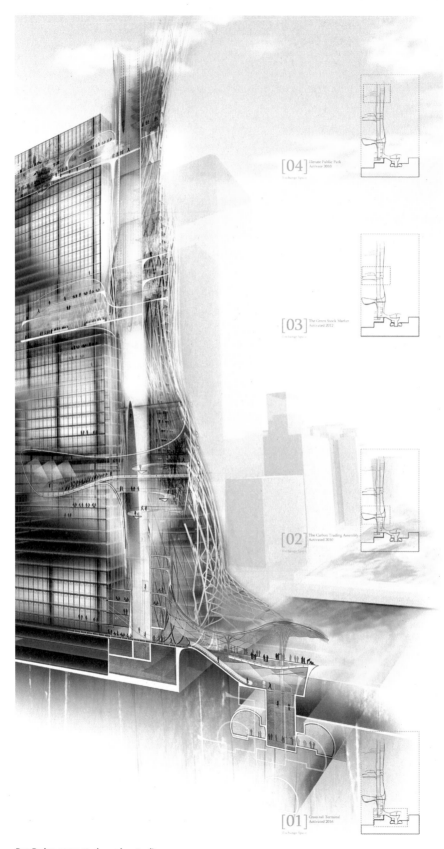

Ben Burley, green stock – carbon trading

MAciej Woroniecki, floating infrastructure

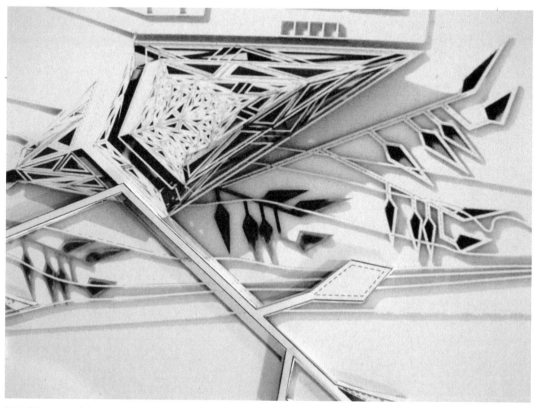

Selina Bolton, water infrastructure

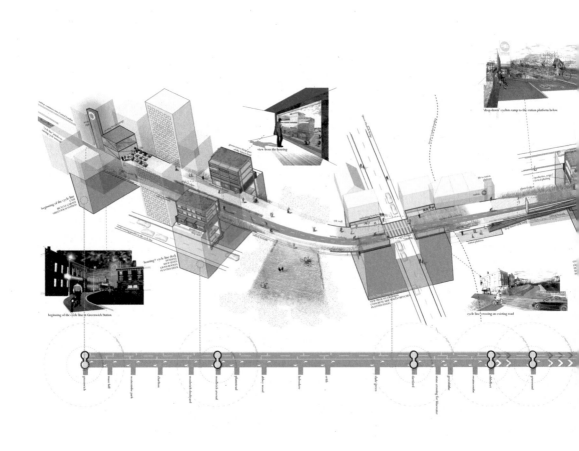

Mellis Haward, long section of cycle line – green infrastructure

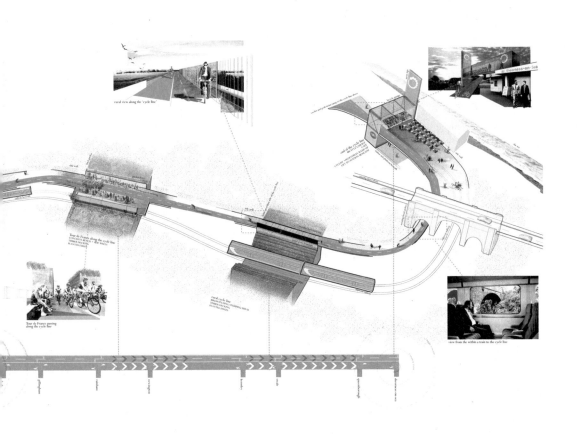

rural view along the 'cycle line'

Tour de France along the cycle line

Tour de France passing along the cycle line

rural cycle line

view from the within a train to the cycle line

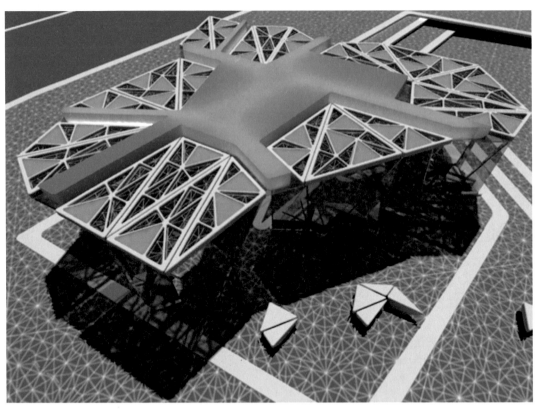

Schweitzer urban development, Brussels – participation pavilion rendering, B612/T2. Photo B612

Schweitzer Square development, Brussels – participation pavilion build up, B612/T2. Photo B612

Schweitzer Square development, Brussels – workshop with local schools, B612/T2. Photo B612

Schweitzer Square development, Brussels – masterplan model. Photo B612

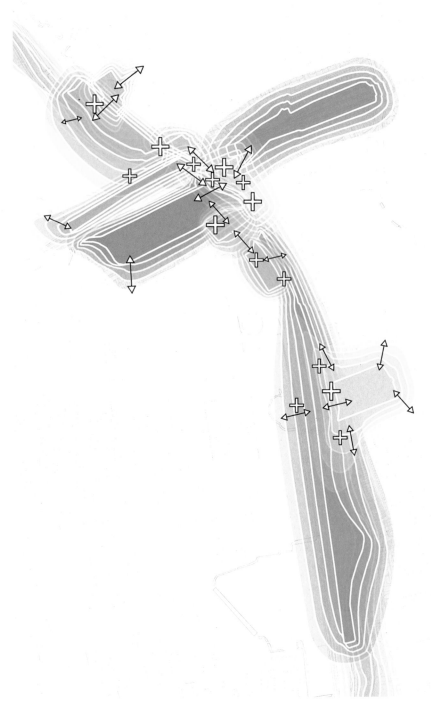

Overlapping frequency diagram for the River Roding development in Ilford – JL Gibbons & T2 spatialwork

Redbridge installation – Uphall Park realisation, JLG/T2, Ilford framework study. Photos Johanna Gibbons

Dip14's Philosophy of the Object

Dip14's Philosophy of the Object

Nina Power

What can a philosopher teach an architect about things? What can a philosopher learn from an architect about objects? Working with Dip14 students proved to be an interesting lesson in how to do things with images rather than words. While I would dogmatically reiterate the importance of explaining oneself effectively, of using words appropriately and (at a more banal level) spelling them correctly in presentations, I was conscious of the fact that all around me there were minds working in extremely different ways to mine, generating visual universes that opened up totally new perspectives on the philosophy of the object. Trying to think about objects together, rather than from the distinct standpoints of our own disciplines, we took our cue from the kind of argument recently put forward by one of our best living object-oriented philosophers, Graham Harman, who speaks of objects in the following (very beautiful) way:

> ...entities roam across the cosmos, inflicting blessings and punishments on everything they touch, perishing without a trace or spreading their powers further – as if a million animals had broken free from a zoo in some Tibetan cosmology. Will philosophy remain satisfied with not addressing any of these objects by name, so as to confine itself to a 'more general' discussion of the condition of the condition of the condition of possibility of ever referring to them? Will philosophy continue to lump together monkeys, tornadoes, diamonds, and oil under the single heading of that-which-lies-outside? Or is there some possibility of an object-oriented philosophy, a sort of alchemy for describing the transformations of one entity into another, for outlining the ways in which they seduce or destroy humans and non-humans alike?[1]

Dip14 were indeed guided by the idea of concocting this 'sort of alchemy'. When we looked back to the atomists, we noted that 'however solid objects seem, they yet are formed of matter mixed with void' (Lucretius, *On the Nature of Things*). The projects were not simply guided by what we could see, by the way buildings impose themselves on the bodies that observe them and walk through them, but by the 'voids' between solids, the 'atmospheres' to which Peter Sloterdijk has referred, and by the need to do justice to every element of a given architectural situation, whether it be water-based, land-based, overground, underground or a curious combination of all four, as many of the projects were.

But what precisely *is* a philosophy of the object? Recently we have seen the revival of older thinking about the object (atomism, a certain type of Leibnizianism, and the ideas of Whitehead and Baudrillard) as well as a celebration of object-philosophy in the present (by such figures as Bruno Latour and Graham Harman). Although approaches that focus on the embodied experience of the world or on the meaning that subjects attach to buildings (or 'dwellings' as Heidegger would say) remain popular within architecture, there is an increasingly strong sense in which we need to include as many 'objects' as possible as participants in our thinking. Environmental concerns in particular have highlighted the need to think of other 'agents' within a network, not simply human actors, but such factors as weather, materials and sustainability. Of course, architecture on some level has always had to think about the objects that it uses and creates, but questioning the implications of all of its participants (human and non-human) is perhaps something that is relatively new, at least in its holistic conception of the environmental impact of such projects.

1. Graham Harman, 'Object-Oriented Philosophy', 1999, can be found at: www.beyng.com/oop.html

The concept of the *actant* has been particularly important for the philosophy of the object undertaken by members of the Dip14 programme. What are *actants*? Anything that participates in a network, we might say, anything that forms a relation with something else, be it human, non-human, structural, linguistic, atmospheric, real or ideal. Going beyond a mere philosophy of objects, we spoke about an object-politics and what happens if you start treating every element of a project as an equal member of the process, something that we could call, following Latour, a 'parliament of things'. What could this parliament be? Who sits in it? Is object-oriented philosophy inherently democratic? Once we turn away from the self-regarding human subject (whether it be the arrogant architect-genius or the haughty philosopher-king), do we automatically accord equal footing to all the objects in a given situation?

When one of the Dip14 students, Ben Burley, included in an early version of his project the half-submerged shopping trolleys that line the banks of the Thames Gateway, were we to understand that these were really equal participants in the complex negotiations that characterise any architectural intervention? Well, yes: the trolleys were not isolated objects (however strangely alluring they looked half-buried in the mud) but part of a system of mediations that included the users of the nearby supermarket, the distances between the supermarket car park and the riverbank, the mixed feelings of pride and despair of local residents and the entry angle between the trolley and its final resting place.

There may of course be an element of the absurd in attempting to enumerate every entity (and their relations) in a scenario, something along the lines of Borges' 'Chinese encyclopedia', where animals are divided into:

> (a) those that belong to the Emperor; (b) embalmed ones; (c) those that are trained; (d) suckling pigs; (e) mermaids; (f) fabulous ones; (g) stray dogs; (h) those included in the present classification; (i) those that tremble as if they were mad; (j) innumerable ones; (k) those drawn with a very fine camel-hair brush; (l) others; (m) those that have just broken a flower vase; (n) those that from a long way off resemble flies. [2]

However, this attempt to give objects and relations their due has some remarkably impressive results. MAciej Woroniecki's 'Waterborne Place', for example, treats river sediment and local residents as equal stakeholders in an ongoing project of long-term sustainable urban regeneration, by expanding the notion of 'lobbying' to reflect fully the 'parliament of things'. As a consequence, his project is visually and politically harmonious and admirably sympathetic to both the natural and the social needs of *actants* living in the vicinity of the waterborne place. In as environmentally and socially diverse an area as the Thames Gateway such an approach can only benefit all the residents, whether they have official residence papers or not.

When Baudrillard in *The System of Objects* talks about the 'luxuriant growth of objects', we should understand this to mean not only the man-made ones (such as Ben's shopping trolleys) nor the natural ones (the sandbank in which they resided), but both, as well as their relation to one another. In this way, the Dip14 programme did material justice to phrases so often bandied around in a lightweight, meaningless way, such as the 'exchange of ideas' or 'stakeholder participation'. When the architect (and the philosopher) become merely one more object in a series of complex negotiations, then any attempt at superiority is undermined from the outset. In this regard, the Dip14 students pursued a variety of thoughtful ways of understanding, accommodating and ultimately helping the Thames Gateway, and through their humility achieved grand results.

2. Jorge Luis Borges, 'The Analytical Language
    of John Wilkins', *Other Inquisitions 1937–1952*
    (Austin: University of Texas Press, 1993).

Communicating Strategies I–IV: Workshops with Marc Angélil at ETH Zurich

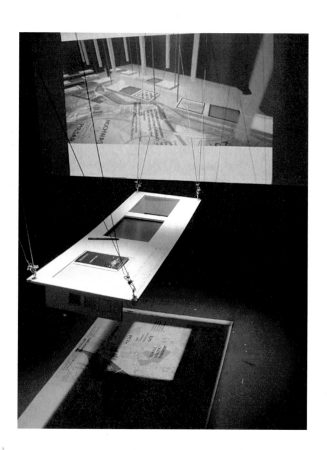

Communicating Strategies I–IV: Workshops with Marc Angélil at ETH Zurich

Interviewed by Peter Staub

Over a period of five years, AADip14 (and its predecessor Dip 9) held four workshops in conjunction with Marc Angélil's MAS programme at the ETH in Zurich. During intensive, week-long collaborations, proposals for interventions on the ETH Campus were developed. Interactive installations challenging the traditional techniques and modes of architectural representation were at the heart of these guerrilla projects. Collaborations between AA and ETH students and staff took on a variety of forms: one year, teams made up of students from both institutions designed and built site-specific installations, while on other occasions AA students developed mediating instruments in order to communicate design proposals created by ETH students. The results were often surprising, for designers and users alike, as through sometimes unconscious interaction the installation turned the user into a performer. In 2006, for example, one group simply amplified the sound made when pressing the buttons on the only cash machine on campus so that it was audible throughout the building. Not only did this challenge the user's privacy, it also changed the immediate atmosphere of the hall while highlighting user frequencies and movement patterns.

AADip14 feels that traditional representation techniques in architecture, such as scale drawings, plans and sections, do not allow any form of intelligent exchange with whoever consults them. In addition, most software used in architectural design is somewhat prescriptive, resulting in strong similarities across the industry. Consequently, we are trying to develop architecture that enables interaction with its users, as well as the tools that are required to design it.

Peter Staub The architect is often the mediating link between clients, contractors, consultants and the public. Where do you think the difficulties in successfully communicating a design proposal lie?

Marc Angélil Communication implies participation – the active involvement and empowerment of manifold actors in a negotiation process. The various parties involved in such an endeavour do not necessarily share the same ideology. Different interests collide. One of the responsibilities of the architect as mediator is to unravel the disagreements between firmly entrenched groups. Here, the question of power and how to overcome the difficulties associated with exerted authority, played out supremacy and exercised control – foregrounding one voice over another – move to the forefront of the debate. Where power enters the game, mediation is generally compromised. Architects, urban designers, and territorial planners repeatedly encounter such moments in the course of their work. Though rarely addressed within the discipline of architecture, power has a determining effect on both the structure of processes and the design outcome. Form follows power. Such a proposition reframes the very understanding of architecture as a field primarily focusing on questions of space, formal expression, context, programme or construction. Notwithstanding the value of such themes, architecture must engage in a discourse on the prevailing economic and political mechanisms at work in the production of physical and social environments. A preoccupation with space requires a discussion on the political economy of space. Similarly, contextual and technological aspects need to be viewed in terms of their socio-economic implications. Design is an inherently political process.

PS Given that the architect's design has to be communicated to a variety of stakeholders often using a different set of tools, how can we improve efficiency in transmitting a proposal?

MA Design cannot exclusively promote a one-way transfer of information, in the sense of communicating a final proposal, but must engage people in a joint dialogue. Discussion and negotiation are part of such an exchange – consensus being the objective. Here, design includes the design of processes. Architects, however, have the tendency to be product-absorbed: the authored and pristine building as the object of desire.

I am not arguing against such an established mode of operation. On the contrary, such an obsession needs to be deployed within an understanding of architecture as a forum in which personal or collective preferences, positions and interests are bartered. Design products, ie projects, plans, models, images, animations, interactive devices and so forth, can be considered tools to be invested in mediation processes – in order to collaboratively raise awareness of specific problems, to devise strategies of how to potentially proceed, and to circumscribe explicit solutions. Traditional or new design instruments can do the job. Design is accordingly an agent in the process. To borrow a concept from Bruno Latour's Actor Network Theory, not solely people but also objects are participants in a course of action. Items of design representation are such objects.

PS In your own experience, how does the design process compare to 30 years ago, with particular reference to communication and presentation of a project? The role of the architect appears to have changed in recent years. During the design process, architects are strongly embedded in a network of specialists. Their job description is more far-reaching than it used to be, and their main task is one of a mediator rather than a designer. What are your views on this shift in roles?

MA New challenges have reframed the profession during the last decades, both in view of qualitative and quantitative demands. We are currently operating in highly complex conditions within social and physical contexts that are marked by conflict, contradiction and discontinuity. Additionally, the scale of the operation has generally changed in terms of the multitude of parameters that need to be addressed – exigencies driven by speed, large numbers and size. Such circumstances have altered the scope and methods of the architect's work. Interdisciplinary team collaboration and stakeholder participation, for example, have moved to the forefront of architectural practice in order to tackle the multifaceted factors circumscribing a task.

Such work requires specific forms of communication as well as organisational structures that guide the transfer of information between fields of knowledge on the one hand (sociology, economy, environmental sciences, etc) and involved parties on the other (clients, city officials, local associations, etc). Here, the architect must be at the centre of any mediation effort. The architect's design expertise must be upheld. This responsibility cannot by any means be given away. I do not believe that project managers, client representatives, or engineers should take on the task. Design must be the decisive platform where all contributions merge. Accordingly, the means of design representation form the necessary instruments to engender decision-making and set the course of action.

PS Is the trend to emphasise the intelligent articulation of a project reflected in architectural education today? How can we as educators provide a better grounding for future architects in communication without sacrificing their skills as designers?

MA Design must be the focal point of architecture education. Rather than considering communication as a supplement, one could argue that design constitutes in itself a form of communicative action, to borrow an expression by Jürgen Habermas. Considering that the means deployed in a process have a determining effect on the product, visualisation techniques – understood as design notations of intentions – play a fundamental role in determining architecture. Here, we need to distinguish between various types of design communication that ought to be part of an educational curriculum.

First, visualisation techniques are needed by the designer to develop a design – what could be termed a kind of auto-communication constantly at work while producing a project. The means and methods must vary during the process. They might include both analogue and digital techniques – models, drawings, texts, diagrams, film clips, organisational charts, cost calculations, etc. In order to promote inspired work, shifts from one technique to another are necessary – an aspect often neglected in teaching.

Second, communication inside the discipline of architecture must be promoted – call it an intradisciplinary form of design communication. Take a position! Argue! Situate your proposition within the history of ideas! Write! Frame a discourse! Design evolves here as a form of research, its objective being the advancement of knowledge. Design research often operates at the edges of architecture and on the thresholds to other fields.

Third, communication with other disciplines needs to be fostered as part of the didactic framework of the design studio. Beyond giving mere lip-service to such a concept, universities today are obliged to practise extra-disciplinary exchanges, going beyond conventionally established boundaries of a given field of endeavour. The integration of findings from other domains is key for the development of a piece of architecture, where design as a discursive platform fulfils a vital task.

Fourth, communication with stakeholders – outside the academic framework – situates design in yet another context. Questions pertaining to participatory processes should be raised within teaching, addressing both the potential as well as drawbacks of such a form of discourse. Fifth, one could go on …

PS What do you think architecture could learn from advertising and new media with regard to both its tools of representation and its communication strategies?

MA Notwithstanding the fact that one could learn something from anything and despite my plea for transdisciplinary interaction, you might be surprised by my answer: generally speaking, nothing. Let me rephrase the question: What should architecture not learn from the mechanism and strategies of the advertising industry? Seduction, the manufacturing of make-believe truths and the promotion of ideal life-styles – endlessly packaged to lure potential buyers – do not necessarily constitute intrinsic values that need be transferred to architecture. This is not to say that one should not look at advertising in order to develop a critical stance. A transfer of techniques implies, within this context, a transfer of ideology. The tools deployed in advertising are not value-free. On the other hand, new media might be another story. Here, one can operate at a more abstract level. The frame of reference associated with new media – as used within the arts, documentary film, scientific research, etc. – leaves room for interpretation and can thus, without being tied to specific sets of beliefs, more easily be transferred to architecture.

PS Inviting stakeholders to participate in a design process has become more and more popular. The voicing of their opinions is mainly restricted to consultation events, exhibitions and questionnaires. Simultaneously, most participants are not trained architects and planners and their opinions are often subjective. Do you think the planning process should encourage participation from third parties?

MA Participation needs to be promoted not as a popular fashion but as a political principal. Who should be involved? How is the process to be structured? Why the task? What should the outcome be? When should something happen? And, since we are talking about architecture and urbanism, where shall the spatial interventions occur? These questions need to be addressed at the very beginning of the undertaking to avoid confusions and possibly reduce the degree of entropy. Additionally, a moderator with knowledge and experience in the field must guide the process. The necessary preparatory work by the experts – architects, urban designers, regional planners, traffic engineers, etc. – establishes through design the foundations for participatory work.

In spite of the complexity of such an enterprise, all this appears more or less simple when working in small groups. The difficulties increase exponentially the more people are involved. How shall participation be organised in metropolitan regions with millions of inhabitants? This is where planning as a collective enterprise begins to exhibit characteristics of state organisations – democracy, for example, as a form of government in which citizens are directly or indirectly empowered.

PS If so, how do you think participatory planning could be designed to be more democratic? Democratic decisions often result in compromises. In architecture this can lead to mediocrity. Can you foresee a planning process that facilitates for both democratic design decisions and good design?

MA Considering that it is nearly impossible to involve large numbers of stakeholders directly, we need to take recourse to the system of political representation. What interest groups exist and who could act on their behalf? These agents are the ones that should partake in the process. Their responsibility is to represent their constituencies, maintain the flow of information, act in the group's best interests, and redirect collectively held opinions.

When the game begins, the representatives become players in a complex set of procedures that cannot be controlled in advance, for participation is by no means a clean-edged affair. As within political democracy, such a course of action might result in compromises and lead to mediocrity. This is where the expert system enters the picture. It is the responsibility of the designers to offer professional judgement. Their obligation is not only to mediate between interest groups but also to consolidate the know-how of manifold disciplines by means of design propositions. Design is ultimately the vehicle to promote both democratic decision-making and 'good design', to use your expression.

PS Given the current global financial crisis, many architectural projects are being scaled down and/or planning is being put on hold. However, difficult times also present opportunities to radically rethink and challenge architectural standards and processes. In your opinion, which aspect of the architectural planning process needs to be addressed most urgently?

MA What needs to be addressed urgently has little to do with architecture but with the predominant system of neoliberal political economy that has engulfed the globe within the last decades – giving priority to the private sector over public interests. The established mechanisms at work have contributed to a general transfer of wealth from the collective to a privileged class and strengthened the consolidation of power in the hands of a chosen few. Such a development has at last been proven to be significantly deficient. The current opportunity entails a general overhaul of the political economy, a radical redirection of objectives from self-seeking individual greed to a society based on solidarity. Architecture and its associated disciplines have the power to make a contribution through design as a platform of collective action – a chance that should not be missed.

AADip14 @ ETH Zurich – Mediating Strategies 2007 (with Marc Angélil): alternative modes of interaction and opinion-gathering

AADip14 @ ETH Zurich – Mediating Strategies 2007 (with Marc Angélil): guerrilla installations on the campus

AADip14 @ ETH Zurich – Mediating Strategies 2008: elements in the user guide can be used as keys to access additional information

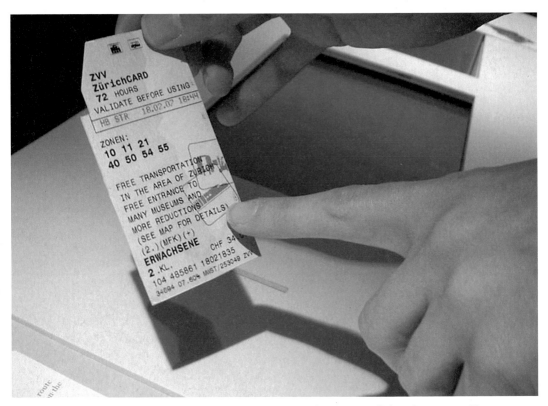

AADip14 @ ETH Zurich – Mediating Strategies 2008: stamping the ticket triggers the appearance of information on screen while leaving a physical mark of interaction

Ever After: A Conversation with AADip14 Graduates

Ever After: A Conversation with AADip14 Graduates

21 January 2011

The aim of the unit was always to give students the tools and methods to start an interesting career in architecture. So for this book a follow-up seemed like an obvious thing to do, to see where they are now and what they have absorbed from the work they did in Diploma 14.

Max Babbe
Moe Ekapob S
Levent Kerimol
Celina Martinez-Cañavate
Peter Staub

Ben Burley
Mellis Haward
Theo Lorenz
Richa Mukhia
MAciej Woroniecki

TL   A few years have passsed since you all finished your diplomas within AADip14. Most of you have been working now for over two years in various fields of architecture, both in London and abroad. The unit's focus on applied work in the urban context and the declared aim of preparing you to start your careers as designers makes it very relevant for us to see how your work within the unit influenced your individual paths. I wanted to ask, what is the first thing that comes to mind when you think about the unit?

MB   A rational and interesting way of thinking about the world around us and how we engage with it.

MW   Accountability. With the work we produced and the topics we tackled there was always an attempt to take into account as many actants and as much of the wider project context as possible.

MH   I remember struggling with the aims of the studio but enjoying the camaraderie between students and the challenge of connecting the academic realm to the professional world.

ES   For me it was collaboration.

BB   And the people… there was such an interesting mix of agendas and preoccupations; it was interesting that the unit structure allowed individuals to follow such diverse lines of enquiry.

PS   If you had to summarise AADip14 in three words, what would they be?

MW   Mediation, collaboration, responsibility.

LK   Plastic boxes, flash scripting and networks.

CM   Networks, collaborative platforms, communication tools.

ES   Just one word: collaboration.

BB   In my case: barcodes, algae and not so interactive design.

RM   Representation, experimentation, participation.

TL   Often when I meet one of you now, you say that finally you really understand what the unit was teaching you. Reflecting on your work at the AA, what parts are now most relevant to you? And what ones do you feel should have been explored more?

MH   The relevance of the unit's work to my current professional life is that it gave me a general critical understanding of architecture/urban planning within the melting pot of political, economic and social networks.

LK   There was always a sense, perhaps, that under all the complex jargon, everything the unit was on about was actually pretty simple. It took many nights of tearing your hair out to be sure of that.
　　　　It was all relevant, both in terms of the things I taught myself, and the larger theoretical framework we operated within. I am constantly finding examples of the things the unit was really about. However I don't think we were ever able to explain the common thought process that ran through the unit – it probably appeared as a disparate collection of random projects to anyone in one of the more formal units. Perhaps this book is the way to tell that story.
　　　　The other thing that could have been explored more is how the utter neutrality of much of network theory negotiation doesn't mean much if there isn't conflict. Power and intent have to come into it in a much bigger way.

MW   I would like to say that mediation is something important, but my personal architectural direction is too strong to allow for too much meddling. Collaboration is an aspect that comes into play every day, which is inevitable, but it's more the way in which I collaborate that I find is directly influenced by my time in Dip14.
　　　　A strong working relationship with a variety of creative disciplines is vital to producing a well-received and animated design proposal and product.

CM   Nowadays architectural projects are still regularly presented to different people in one specific linear way, usually through plans, drawings and some visualisations. But what are other more productive ways to communicate an idea? And how can the same idea communicate differently to the project's various stakeholders? These questions have always been crucial to unit 14 and I have been trying to respond to them in my professional practice.

ES   Again: collaboration. I believe collaboration is a very important aspect in the architectural design discipline and applicable to projects of any scale. One benefit that I found when working on a project collaboratively concerns the integration of sustainable design and long-term development. Collaborating with different parties involved in the project is always beneficial for everyone: the private sector and financial side, the government for the rules and regulations, me professionally and academically and, most importantly, the public. Vertical collaboration and mass collaboration also helps in terms of sharing, informing and expanding knowledge and pushing the ideas and concepts forward and getting support and approval from all sides. The incorporation of technology for real-time collaborative platforms also helps me to approach design thinking in a different way, from the initial briefing, consultants' meeting, to proposal presentation and on, after the project completion, for future development.

In addition, I ask my students to approach their projects through an investigation of the notion and potential of 'architectural production' by looking at all aspects of architecture beyond just the design side of it. The idea of a collaborative approach becomes a logical discussion when looking at architecture's close relationship to other industry and disciplines such as engineering, construction and real-estate.

MB   The way relationships are experienced. To a certain extent I agree with Lev, the 'realness' was difficult to grasp when the project was set up for us at the AA. The urgency and reality of practice sharpen the view and bring to light the importance of the work of Dip14. Also, building on experiences in practice and working with a wide range of consultants, my influence on smaller projects is proportionally greater, and more easily measured.

TL   One of the main aims of Dip14 was always to teach a method of working that would help to start your career as a professional rather than merely offer specific tools or styles. What do you think you have taken into your professional life from this approach of the unit?

RM   No ivory towers at Dip14! The unit demanded that we engage in live projects, which inherently meant dealing with super-complicated issues that in most units you could probably ignore or rationalise. Dip14 encouraged us to fully embrace the messy real world, which has proved to be great preparation for professional life, developing the ability to work though complex issues and instilling confidence in our role as designers.

LK   I always liked the phrase 'designing the design process'. Perhaps I've misused it, but it has been useful to reassure myself that all the meetings and emails and daily drudgery are still design. I have never been a strong believer in style, or overly complex tools. 'Process', to me, does not mean a technical procedure or methodological recipe of how to design a building. It is the messy reality of making things happen, and persuading and convincing, arranging funding and arranging people, which is what we actually do.

Dip14 was good because it allowed an unusually large degree of freedom to pursue the topics we were interested in. The theoretical framework could be pushed and pulled, manipulated and put to your own ends. This openness of the tutors helped build my confidence in my ideas and make me certain these were things I wanted to pursue. And this is the most valuable thing about diploma – forget about pass or fail – it's self-belief.

BB   Communication is essential in what we do as designers; the work of the unit showed the necessity to tailor how and what we present to the various stakeholders of a project.

MH   This was a successful aspect of the unit and the work I now do takes this approach to every project. We work without a house style, but with the ability to adapt to the many roles an architect takes on.

MB   A highly analytical approach, combining, linking and mediating between people, products and methods of construction – seeing where efficiencies can be made or methods synthesised to create something that is better and more interesting.

MW   Judging each design element beyond its designed context. The moment you set a footprint, a site boundary, or even a line within which you will design, you have to be responsible for the future impact of that line. I definitely took a sense of responsibility from our unit work into my professional work, which possibly accounts for my frequent feelings of guilt.

CM   Although design is often characterised as a process of creating a product, it is also very much a social process in which communication plays a critical role. Designers must communicate both with users and with the organisation of which they are part. To do collaborative work in an interdisciplinary environment has been very important to unit 14's agenda and it is still very relevant in my work today.

TL   In some cases it seems that you've been able to take the agenda you set in the unit further within your own practice, as with the topic of the 'Green Grid', the 'self-build' developments or environmental issue. Could you give some brief examples of where this happened? Were they successful or a failure (or both)?

MW   Collaboration is for sure something that I fell comfortably into because of our unit work. In terms of 'topic', I have managed to push further some technical aspects of my diploma work dealing with sedimentation, in the development of public space along a tidal canal development.

CM   In most of the projects I have been working on, interdisciplinary meetings, workshops and informative events have been essential to successful outcomes.

ES   Yes, collaboration in both teaching and practice for every possible chance that I have.

MH   Continuous networks of infrastructure, a topic in my unit project, has been on the agenda within Gort Scott's publication 'London's High Streets', a research document on behalf of the London Development Agency and in collaboration with UCL's digital mapping team, cataloguing and analysing the continuous 'necklaces' of high streets across the city.

LK   Following on from your previous question, I strived for a huge amount of realism in my diploma work, to make it actually do-able. Although Theo might claim they were 'actually applied' I don't think anyone really got there. They were inevitably student projects, and therefore slightly more theoretical, or more naïve, depending on how you look at it. But I had a real commitment to the potential for application, mixed with something too ambitious to consider exploring outside of academia.

There is some support for things like self-build and alternative models of development in public sector regeneration circles. However the need for wide-ranging culture change is a huge hurdle and will take a long time to shift. Added to this is the difficulty of minimising the inevitable problems such experimental approaches will have in the early days, where they co-exist with more conventional methods. I spent a lot of time designing processes to minimise negative consequences and set up the likelihood of something good happening. But it would be risky to promote self-build as an idea on its own, if the subtleties of the work were shed along the way. Dumbing down or manipulation for other interests than my own is a real risk – much like recent pronouncements by the Con-Dem coalition on the big society, localism and open source planning, which are deeply troubling in detail, even though I might believe in them as principles. In the wrong hands these ideas can do more harm than good, so it's dangerous to release them and simply hope for the best.

Having said that, in some of the developments I'm working on in the Albert Basin and North Woolwich we are encouraging development partners to look at self-build and other more innovative forms of development. These will probably be relatively token gestures which don't have much to do with my diploma work, but I suppose it is some progress in that task of culture change. I sometimes think I might have more success in changing the development industry as a surveyor.

I'll let Richa talk about Green Grid, even though I spent a lot of time working on the large-scale strategy version at Design for London. While I'm frequently told this is an amazing project in many ways, I always felt it was crude at this scale compared to Richa's work. I suppose some of the work we've been doing with muf architecture/art and J&L Gibbons in Dalston and some of the smaller interventions in the Albert Basin are more in tune with Richa's work. Green Grid is more of a marketing wrapper to galvanise political support and marshal financial resources. What do you think Richa?

RM I agree that the Green Grid and some of the other large-scale politically driven projects that Dip14 investigated prove to be disappointingly rigid when one deals with them in practice. Within the unit we had the freedom to challenge preconceptions (both our own and the policy-makers') in a way that doesn't happen in practice. My own experience with the Green Grid project as both a student and someone involved in the delivery has shown that it is difficult for those involved in the live projects to re-imagine the potential of the opportunity.

TL Mediation of architecture and with it the process of negotiation of design was a core part of the unit. Do you have in your practice any applied examples where this took place, be it in the form of client negotiation, public participation or exhibitions in relation to the proposed projects?

LK All the time, there are far too many to mention. The public sector and the 'state' are completely non-homogeneous; add to that the private sector and politicians, and you have everyone pulling in different directions, performing all sorts of manoeuvres. Larry Barth said in one of my first crits that a large corporation can have about 20 motives at any one time – it's not always about profit maximisation, there can be long-term views, of increasing market share, or promotion. It's a miracle that organisations are able to act corporately, and you realise that a large part of bureaucracy is in place to stop individuals in an organisation acting individually. However the complex manoeuvring and negotiation is always there and can't be eliminated, to the extent that you begin to wonder what if there was no bureaucratic power structure holding these corporations together, could negotiation keep things working?
So I don't think negotiation is unique to Dip14 or to architecture. Everyone does it. All the time. It even takes place within the individual mind.

RM I happen to have been involved in many such processes from hands-on 'charrette' workshops to debates around planning policy and a formal public enquiry on parts of the new London Plan. But as Lev says, this is something that we all do all the time. I suppose it helps to be conscious of our role in the process.

ES Yes, the collaboration process helps when negotiating with other parties involved in the design project.

MH Negotiation, exhibition and public participation are the constant challenges and delights of my work, whether face to face with the public of Walthamstow using simple maps on the street, with contractors on site or exhibiting to your professional peer group.

MW All of my projects to date have followed intense and hectic schedules not allowing for much public participation. It was always quite a contradiction for me, in terms of the unit's 'public approach' and push towards participation. It was a struggle, because even though participation and a public response is informative and in many cases a necessary, part of the design process, I wanted no response from the public. After spending months progressing a design, adapting and reassessing its logic, the last thing I would want to do is receive public comment on an academic, architectural project. I feel there are certain projects which should be untouched, for danger of being diluted. Social comment has its place in the architectural design process, as architects have a responsibility in what they produce. I will use one building as an example: the Guangzhou Opera. Someone should be held accountable.

CM Yes, I have been working on a large housing project in the Canton of Berne in Switzerland where the existing neighbourhoods have been actively involved in participative workshops and informative events throughout the whole design process.

BB Negotiation filters through every part of the design process from client consultations and is equally importantly in the studio.

ES Mediation is very helpful when trying to resolve the differences in the design proposal, especially at the urban design and planning scale.

CM Mediation should be a guiding principle not only at the beginning and throughout the process of a project but also after planning has 'finished'. In other words, the success of prospective projects depends on communicating/mediating its overall intentions not only for a short-term outcome but also for a long-term vision.

MB Mediation cannot be forced out of people, as a guiding principle. It is more of a cultural construct. Mediating needs to become natural, fluid and easily digestible and fun if it is going to have a real impact in our built environment.

BB The lack or negotiation, or mediation that seems to so frequently occur between one boundary of development and the next leaves both physical and social edges overlooked and forgotten. One essential role of urban design and planning is to assist and steer the designs so that individual projects are successfully stitched into the pubic realm and work together as a coherent piece of urban fabric.

TL The unit always had a strong link to philosophy and in particular the philosophy of the object. Today it seems that Latour, Sloterdijk and other scholars are again more widely discussed in architecture. Do you follow this discussion and what do you take from it?

ES   Latour is becoming one of the main topics in the design studio that I'm teaching. A lot of the discussion revolves around his social criticism and construct; we also try to relate the reading to the context of Bangkok and development in this region.

LK   I thought Latour was easier to understand than Sloterdijk. I'm pretty interested in philosophy and science and anything that involves abstract thought, so I enjoy them as intellectual challenges. But I do not mourn the passing of the 90s fad of quoting bits of Deleuze or Derrida out of context as an excuse to make a funky-shaped building. In the same way I find other forms of artistic inspiration a diversion. Inspiration and design emerge from the social and historical context, and pragmatic process of making buildings and shaping places.

MW   I am starting to reignite these discussions with colleagues of mine who have used the financial crisis to return to university and use the time to learn new skills and approaches. In some cases they have chosen more theoretical courses which delve deep into Heidegger, which makes for interesting discussion.

PS   Through this book, your work is now part of this discussion too. What role do books/the written word have in architecture? And how important are they in your work?

ES   It's very important if it's a well-constructed argument and I believe writing should be part of the architectural design proposal.

LK   I want to read more books, but hardly ever have time. Sometimes I think of quitting my job to spend a year reading and writing. Blogs and twitter are becoming more important for me too, but again it feels as though there is so much out there that is interesting that I never feel like I'm getting everything out of them.

MW   Active discussions, documented works and new approaches are essential to push new architectures forward, be it through printed and bound media or online documents.

CM   I think reading as well as writing is a very helpful and essential tool in the design process of any project. Nevertheless I do not use it enough.

TL   To what extent are you still using the methods of representation we used within the unit, such as exploded drawings, X-D drawing or interactive models or installations?

PS   Have you developed new modes of representation based on the above?

LK   Not really, I guess it's still the diagram and diagrammatic maps. I've got quite into the nuances of mapping and the representation of statistics, which are about clarity and simplicity and conventions. Although some of the drawings in the unit are able to achieve this clarity, often there is a tendency for it to be overridden with complexity for its own sake – as if this somehow looks more sexy. I don't think the architect's struggle to communicate will be cured by inventing new methods of representation. These seem to reinforce the introverted dialogue of pretentious architects doing intellectual acrobatics, and require a huge number of words to explain. I think it's about really understanding graphic design and drawing conventions. In my experience a pen sketch communicates a lot more, and we shouldn't be afraid to admit we need to learn this.

ES   We developed new modes of representation based on the unit methods. One of the modes of representation that we are currently exploring is with mobile platforms and technology.

MH   Interactive installations in their most stripped down form are often used within my firm's urban design strategy work, with simple stickers and post-its, or a basic online questionnaire. The aim is not necessarily to collate finite data but as a catalyst for invaluable discussion.

ES   Also, you can't beat an exploded axo to explain a tricky detail on site!

MW   I am still using my method of drawing with motion and programmatic change. I am pushing to add time as a layer into my drawings.

BB   More recently, while working on music and concert buildings, we've found ourselves collaborating with acoustically adept clients, so as well as presenting schemes through models, drawings and visualisations we have tried to accompany them with evocative soundscapes which try to conjure more of the emotive atmosphere of the spaces.

RM   The constant challenging of representational techniques in Dip14 has definitely left its mark! Again the engagement with real projects has meant that even as students we were thinking of the viewers of our representations as non-architects and non-experts leading to an emphasis on clarity and 'direct representation'. I find I now can't help but question the assumed mode of representation for a given task and search for a clearer more direct method.

CM   I often use explosion drawings or relational schemes to represent the different layers of a project.

MB   I am always working in axonometric – exploded wherever possible. Models are key to communicating ideas to a wide range of people. Online collaborative drawing tools, instant messaging, etc...

TL   Some of you are teaching now as well. What methods have you taken from your AA experience and what are you doing differently?

ES I'm using every method from my AA experience. One of the differences is the grading. It's very stupid to evaluate design proposal and thinking through letter grade.

LK I am teaching on a new MA course on Spatial Planning and Urban Design at London Metropolitan University. The aim is to 're-establish the notion of the planner-architect', or at least get more architects working within the public sector, by hopefully getting joint accreditation by RTPI and RIBA. We have the slightly arrogant idea that design is a culture that can only be learnt by doing and gaining experience – you can't learn it from a book. So while you can teach architects to become planners, you can't teach planners to become designers overnight. So the MA is only open to those with undergraduate degrees in architecture. They have design work in the standard diploma units, but they also have a huge amount of seminar-based discussion sessions. I've been responsible for the planning policy and urban economics modules, and have brought in expert guests and set reading tasks, which has been a real education for me too. The approach is not to burden students with too much theory, but to equip them for the world of urban place shaping, with knowledge and examples of practice. The idea of negotiation is a big part of this, but not explicitly stated in theoretical terms. The students are encouraged to join in a broader debate by talking with professionals and by keeping a blog, which has been very useful for many of them, similar to keeping log books at the AA.

MB When visiting Greenwich, it was interesting to see how projects only existed for a moment, whereas our experience in Dip14 taught us that projects were a series of processes that could be unravelled and influenced.

RM I think the freedom afforded to us to develop our projects based on our own interests and preoccupations but structured around the unit's ideology was very important in helping us develop as individuals. I have tried to encourage a similar freedom for my students despite the challenges this poses me now! Another key tool is direct representation and testing ideas at 1:1 scale on site. This seems like a very simple and obvious instrument for architects, however I have found it really difficult to encourage students to engage in this method of testing. They invariably equate success with the level of public engagement, and struggle to appreciate the value of the experiment.

Biographies

Richa Mukhia

Richa graduated from the AA in 2006. Her final diploma project was awarded the AA Honours prize and was shortlisted for the RIBA silver medal. After working for Softroom and Kevin Fellingham Architects, Richa co-curated a major exhibition for the P3 gallery in London. She now works for Design for London where she is involved in masterplans and public realm projects in Lewisham and leads on housing standards work. She is also currently working on a research and development study of suburban housing for Baylight properties that will culminate in a book and exhibition. Richa is also a design tutor at the University of Westminster.

Levent Kerimol

After graduating from the AA in 2007, Levent began working at Design for London, a public-sector organisation linked to the Greater London Authority. He has worked in Rainham, the Albert Basin and the Upper Lea Valley, as well as on the East London Green Grid and Industrial Land Policy. The work involves developing urban strategies, organising funding and other agencies around projects, commissioning consultants, and acting as a design advisor on the client side. Levent is also teaching on the new MA course in Spatial Planning and Urban Design at London Metropolitan University, and continues to contribute to academic conferences and talks, journals and books, while acting as visiting critic in various universities.

Celina Martinez-Cañavate

Celina graduated from the AA in London in 2007 and has since worked on urban planning projects in Zurich- based offices. She completed studies in Interior Design in Madrid and also holds an AA MSc in Sustainable Environmental Design. For the last three years Celina has been working for blue architects and Ruprecht Architekten, where she has been in charge of several competitions for large-scale projects and urban design. She is currently working as a project manager for KCAP architects and planners in Zurich and is also the executive assistant for the Future Cities Laboratory project, a joint five-year research collaboration between the ETH (Eidgenössische Technische Hochschule Zürich), the NUS (National University of Singapore) and the NTU (Nanyang Technological University).

MAciej Woroniecki

MAciej has designed in California, Switzerland and England. After six years of studies at the AA, MAciej graduated in 2008. After finishing the AA, while working for Stephen Spence, MAciej worked on England's tallest bridge, in Sunderland, and saw it through to planning. He has also worked on residential refurbishments in London, apartment buildings in Mumbai, and recently became finalist in an urban design competition in Beirut while working for Martha Schwartz. Currently he is designing a theatre to be built in Wuhan, China, working at Mark Fisher Studio.

Max Babbe

After graduating from the AA in 2006, Max designed his first private house in Jersey, which has been given a number of awards including, most recently, the RIBA Downland Prize. Alongside working in practice, Max was invited to run a series of emerging media lectures, and acted as a visiting technical consultant at the AA for the students of Diploma Unit 14. He has also been a guest critic at Greenwich University at the undergraduate level. Max is continuing his research into digitally augmented networks, working on a number of privately commissioned websites and data management systems. He is currently a project architect at MOOARC running a number of projects including private residences, schools, leisure facilities and commercial developments across Europe.

Moe Ekapob S (Ekapob Sudsukpaisarn) Moe Ekapob S is the design principal and founder of AND Development Co and teaches in the International Programme in Design and Architecture (INDA) at Chulalongkorn University, Bangkok, where he is currently setting up a new Digital Design Division/Laboratory. He graduated from the AA and has since worked at ARUP Advanced Geometry Unit (AGU) in London and SOM in both the Urban Design and Planning Group and the Digital Design Group in New York. He was also part of the design team (IBA) for the recently completed Canton Tower in Guangzhou, China.

Mellis Haward
After graduating from the AA in 2007, Mellis worked with INABA Projects and Jeffrey Inaba on conceptual 'future space' proposals for a global digital software company. In New York she then worked for Pell Overton offices in an installation entitled 'Passive Aggressive' which went on to win New York's Young Architect of the Year. On returning to London in 2008 Mellis worked at Feilden Clegg Bradley Studios working on the construction stage of Leeds Metropolitan University Department of Architecture. She is now working for Gort Scott Architects, where her experience in AADip14 is informing the consultation strategies of urban development projects in East London.

Ben Burley
Having previously worked for the GLA's Architecture + Urbanism Unit on strategic urban design projects and policy in the Thames Gateway, Ben sought on graduation to work for practitioners delivering some of the studies and schemes. Developing interests formed in Dip14, Ben had the opportunity to incorporate strands from his final diploma thesis while working on a zero-carbon, high-density housing scheme on the Olympic Park fringe. This project exposed the challenges of applying and successfully delivering the plethora of environmental policy, renewable energy legislation and sustainable construction techniques into a viable scheme.